Straight To The Source:

A Guide To Dropshipping

Steve Sonnenberg

&

Leah Darrow

developerCo
230 E 400 S
Springville, Ut 84663
publish@developerco.com

First Printing 2011

ISBN:146625372X
ISBN-13:9781466253728

DEDICATION

To every person trying to start a business selling products on the Internet.

Table of Contents

Acknowledgments

I would like to say thank you to Leah Darrow, my writer. I would also like to thank all the people who have ever worked at WholesaleMatch. This book couldn't have been written without all the experiences we have all shared... good or bad. - Steve

Introduction:

Most pitches for dropshipping focus on an image of ease: Make money from home in your underwear! Start selling products this afternoon! Pay off your house by the end of the year! Dropship-retailing is definitely a legitimate way to make an income: it allows you to sell products online without purchasing an extensive inventory. However, like any online business, a dropship-retail business requires education, planning, an investment of time and money, and a lot of hard work.

First, what is dropshipping? Dropshipping is a supply-chain management technique where the retailer does not carry an inventory of products, but rather submits individual orders to a manufacturer or distributor who ships the products directly to the customer. Simply put, a dropship-retailer sells a product like any normal retailer, but when the sale is made, they order the product from a third party and have it shipped to the customer as if it was coming from them. You've probably bought products from a dropship-retailer without even knowing it.

Imagine that you were going to start you own online business this afternoon. Let's say it's an umbrella website. Where would you purchase the umbrellas from? How would you package them? How would you ship them? What would you do to get people to your website in the first place? How would you even set up the website? How do you handle returns? What about filing your taxes at the end of the year?

All these questions and more will be answered in subsequent chapters. This book is designed to teach you how to sell products online. Products for online resale are generally purchased wholesale or from a dropshipper. Both these systems will be examined, as will most other aspects of setting up an online business. From choosing a product to selling on eBay to marketing your website, this book will walk you through the process step by step.

Anyone can start an online business. I've worked with 78 year old grandmothers, 18 year old entrepreneurs, and middle-aged businessmen and women who've operated successful brick-and-mortar businesses for years and are looking to expand into the online market. People's income expectations vary widely: some want to sell a few products on eBay to supplement their holiday funds, while others dream of sailing the Mediterranean on their e-commerce earnings. The money you make from your online business will be directly proportional to the work you put in. Below a certain threshold of dedication and due diligence, you probably won't make money at all, or will lose what you've invested.

For this reason, I urge you to read this book thoroughly so you understand the requirements before you make an investment. Make no mistake, an online business is as serious an undertaking as opening a hair salon or a hardware store. It will take a lot of time and some money. If you don't have any time or money, you should probably re-evaluate your decision to start a business. Your most important investment, the factor that really determines whether you succeed or fail in e-commerce, is your contribution to education. You're going to have to make a lot of decisions, from the color of your logo to the size of your advertising budget. With the proper preparation you can make the right decisions so your online business will soar like a swan instead of sputtering out like the Spruce Goose (or even flaming like the Hindenburg). As my mother-in-law would say, Proper Prior Planning Prevents Piss Poor Performance. I'm here to help with that planning.

Note: If you are planning to embark in e-commerce immediately, you may want to take a minute to read chapter 14, as this chapter includes a checklist to start your online business.

Chapter 1

The Battle Royale: Dropshipping Vs. Wholesaling

Dropshipping vs. Wholesaling is a classic battle, like Coke vs. Pepsi or Mac vs. PC. As in any clash of the Titans, there are positives and negatives to both options. The system that works best for you will probably have a lot to do with your capital and the type of product you want to sell. It is also a question of commitment, rather like the choice between the wife and the minivan full of kids, or the Astin Martin and martinis drunk shaken not stirred.

First, an overview of dropshipping: purchasing your products via dropship is beneficial because it prevents you having to carry an inventory. This means you don't have to make a large initial investment, and you don't have to rent or purchase a warehouse or other space to store your products in. You don't have to buy packing and shipping materials or spend the time to package and mail each order. The lack of manpower required to fulfill orders from a dropshipper means you probably won't have to hire lackeys to assist you with orders. Because you have no inventory, your product line is also extremely flexible: if a particular product isn't selling, you can simply remove the listing from your website or eBay store - you don't have to worry about unloading a bunch of unsold cowboy hats or roller derby skates.

The biggest negative of dropshipping is that you almost never get as good a price as you would purchasing wholesale. I recently contacted a supplier of hand-made bamboo furniture and the difference between dropship and wholesale rates was staggering: their chairs were discounted 75% off retail price when purchased wholesale, but only 25% discounted when purchased via dropship. In general, wholesale products can be purchased for around 50% retail cost, and dropship products for 75% . Dropshippers may also charge fees – from $3 to $20 per order. Depending on the product and order size, this can take a bite out of your profits.

Other issues revolve around supply. When purchasing from a dropshipper, you have much less control over the availability of products. There may be little notice when a dropshipper runs out of a certain product. You have no influence on how much holiday stock they keep on hand, or when they might suddenly change their product line, axing items that have been good sellers for you.

Finally, dropshipping does not give you any control over how the item is shipped, and returns can be a problem. The shipping method may be expensive, or may not offer the security you're looking for. Some dropshippers provide "blind dropshipping", which means their company information is not be visible on the package (you have to check if their name will be on the packing materials or receipt). Some suppliers go so far as to allow you to put your own label or brand on their products (spices, lotions, sunglasses, etc.). Other dropshippers ship your orders exactly like orders from their own company, and customers may be confused when their package arrives with a different business name on it. If there is a problem with the item and the customer wants to return it, some dropshippers allow the customer to ship the item directly back to them, but in other instances it will have to be shipped to you first. If the product is heavy or cumbersome, like a tent, this can be expensive. Dropshippers also tend to have more restrictions on where they will ship their products – if you plan to sell to people outside the United States, you may have a more difficult time finding a dropshipper.

By contrast, purchasing wholesale allows you more control but also requires a larger investment and greater commitment. You'll get your products cheaper, but you'll have to store, package, and mail them. You have to count the time you spend on order fulfillment as costing an actual dollar amount – the phrase "time is money" is not just a cliché. The hours you spend packing and shipping orders are hours that could be invested into other aspects of your business, or used to earn income through another venue. When purchasing wholesale, you may have to make a large initial order (anywhere from $100-3000) or buy products in "packs" or "crates" (six pairs of jeans or a flat of 40 candles). If any of your products don't sell, you're faced with slashing the price or eating the loss.

On the flip side, purchasing wholesale allows you to control your inventory and ensure you have the supply to meet your demand. You also have more flexibility in how you sell your products. Promotional offers like "free shipping on orders over $50" are much easier when you have control over the order and the way it's shipped. You may be able to negotiate bulk shipping discounts with a post office or courier, and you can easily include fliers and promotional materials in your packaging. One of the biggest benefits of doing the order fulfillment yourself is the ability to exercise quality control – you can examine each product you send out and provide extras like a thank you note to your customer or gift wrapping.

Wholesalers are also more flexible than your average dropshipper. Many will allow you to apply for a line of credit if you don't have the cash to make the large initial order they require. Some will allow you to mix and match the color and style of product in quantity orders. Some have no minimum order requirements once the first large order is made. Due to this flexibility, some wholesalers can actually be used as dropshippers – if your wholesaler has a low or nonexistent minimum order requirement for repeat orders, you can buy products singly as sales are made on your website. Sometimes you can even have the product shipped directly to your customer. Thus, if you are intent on using a dropshipper but are having trouble finding a supplier for your particular product, you should look through the available wholesalers - some might actually fulfill the function of a dropshipper to your satisfaction.

When choosing whether to purchase your products via dropship or wholesale, you need to consider a number of factors. First, are you absolutely sure what product you want to sell? Let's go back to our fictional umbrella business. If you are positive that umbrellas are all you want to sell, you've dreamed about it since you got your first Hello Kitty umbrella at the age of six, and you've done the market research so you know there is sufficient demand and not too much supply, then you may want to go ahead and purchase wholesale. If, however, you think you might want to sell umbrellas, but are also considering golf clubs, teddy bears, and power tools, you could test-run all these items on eBay using a dropshipper.

Your second consideration is whether there's a dropship or wholesaler supplier available for your product. While most products can be purchased wholesale, dropshipping is not quite as diffuse. Brand-name products and products from certain industries like clothing/textiles are more frequently sold wholesale. For example, clothing manufacture is generally split into two categories: expensive brand-name clothes that are manufactured by American companies and are only provided for resale to select, high-end retailers, and cheap foreign-made clothing that is sold wholesale. Cheap clothing needs to be sold wholesale because the profit margin for the manufacturer is fairly slim and the distribution structure is low-budget. Jeans, t-shirts, etc., are imported in crates and sold in packs of 20 shirts, 6 pairs of jeans, for extremely low prices – usually only $3-12 per piece. The manufacturer will sell to anyone, small businesses, online retailers, but they don't have the means or the infrastructure to provide dropshipping. If you want to sell a product in an industry where dropshipping is rare, you may have to be more flexible, or focus on a specific product that isn't governed by the same restrictions – say, hostess aprons. Some products aren't available for resale at all: many brand name products have exclusive distribution agreements (i.e. Juicy purses). Sometimes you can get around this by purchasing overstock or refurbished items or replicas/look-alikes. Sometimes you can negotiate with a manufacturer or distributor and convince them to supply you. On occasion, you'll have to pick a different product.

Third, you need to determine whether you can afford to use a wholesaler. Purchasing wholesale simply may not be an option for you because you don't have the capital or credit score for a large initial order. In this case you may want to use a dropshipper for a few months until you've built up enough profits to invest in a wholesale purchase.

Segueing from dropshipping to wholesaling or using a combination of the two systems is often the best option. Using a dropshipper allows you to experiment, to find which products work the best for you: you can test the popularity of your products before making a large commitment to them. In some cases, you may want to use a dropshipper for the majority of your product line, but purchase one extremely popular product wholesale to get a better discount.   Generally I encourage people to sell products from a dropshipper in the initial stages of their online business to get the hang of it, then switch to purchasing wholesale to improve their profit margins.

Before you make any definite decision regarding the dropship vs. wholesale dilemma, I strongly recommend that you make a chart like the one listed below. This can help you to see the difference in profit when purchasing from a dropshipper vs. a wholesaler.   Be aware that buying wholesale is not invariably cheaper than purchasing from a dropshipper, particularly once you add in an hourly wage for the time you would spend packing and shipping your own products. You will need to input precise numbers to determine which supplier will ultimately be the most profitable.

The following chart lists two potential products, sleeping bags and juicers. As you can see, it would be more profitable to purchase the sleeping bags wholesale. Conversely, due to expensive packing materials and shipping fees, one would actually lose money buying and selling the juicers wholesale, so dropshipping is the better option. I'm assuming that my fictional entrepreneur is storing the items in their garage or basement, so there are no storage costs listed.

Sleeping Bags (Retail Price $280):	
Wholesale:	
Purchase Price of Product:	$140.00
Storage Costs:	$0
Packing Materials:	$4.00
Shipping Costs:	$12.00
Time Spent ($15/hour):	1.5 hours= $22.50
Total Cost:	$188.50
Profit:	$91.50
Dropship:	
Purchase Price of Product:	$200.00
Dropship Fees:	$10
Total Cost:	$210.00
Profit:	$70.00
Juicers (Retail Price $99.00)	
Wholesale:	
Purchase Price of Product:	$65.00
Storage Costs:	$0
Packing Materials:	$6.00
Shipping Costs:	$18.00
Time Spent ($15/hour):	1.5 hours =$22.50
Total Cost:	$111.50
Profit:	-($12.50)

Dropship:	
Purchase Price of Product:	$75.00
Dropship Fees:	$2.50
Total Cost:	$77.50
Profit:	$21.50

Chapter 2

How To Beat Wal-Mart: Capturing a Niche Market

In Michael Bergdahl's book *What I Learned from Sam Walton: How to Compete and Thrive in a Wal-Mart World*, he says "The key to competing and surviving against Wal-Mart is to focus your business into a niche or pocket where you can leverage your strengths in the local marketplace." Bergdahl believes that the key to competing with big business is to capture a niche, and I happen to agree. You may think you're not in competition with Wal-Mart, but Wal-Mart symbolizes every mega-retailer who can offer a price and selection far beyond what you will be able to touch with your online business.

This is a common trap that many e-commerce entrepreneurs fall into: when I'm talking to people in the early stages of brainstorming, they say "Well, I figure I'll sell a little bit of everything. I'll have all kinds of stuff on my site, so whatever people need, they can come to me." No, no, and no. Let's get this out in the open right now: you really have no chance of selling your products more cheaply than Wal-Mart does. Wal-Mart can offer rock-bottom prices for a number of reasons: one, they have the bulk-purchasing muscle to strong-arm suppliers into giving them products for ridiculously low prices. Two, they operate their business with scary high-tech German efficiency so not a penny is wasted anywhere, ever. Three, they have a bajillion well-trained employees working on the cheap.

Does this mean you should roll over now, and let everybody buy everything at Wal-Mart? No, because price isn't everything. There are other factors to consider, like customer service, perks, and product selection. By "perks" I mean little extras like free shipping, coupons, free t-shirts, etc., and also informational articles or other value-adders on your website. We'll talk more about these later; what I want to focus on right now is product selection. Wal-Mart may carry everything from sewing supplies to steaks to shoe polish, but they don't offer a great selection in any of these categories. In fact, when I'm buying my 24 Maruchan cup 'o noodles for the month, I have to get them from Macy's because Wal-Mart only carries Chicken, Beef and Shrimp, not the fancy flavors I crave like Chili Lime Chicken and Super Spicy Hot. Since I'm already at Macy's, I do the rest of my shopping. Thus Macy's has triumphed over Wal-Mart with Chili Lime Chicken cup o' noodles.

How can you apply this principle to your online business? Instead of trying to operate a general store, you need to choose a niche market. You can expand to fill all the needs of this niche, completely capturing the market so that Wal-Mart or Best Buy or another other mega-retailer can't compete with your specialized attention.

Products in a niche market by definition do not comply with the strict price competition that rules in a more general market. This is due to "price elasticity of demand" – basically a product that is widely available, has numerous substitutes, or is unnecessary has an elastic demand – when prices are raised, demand falls sharply. A more specialized product with fewer suppliers, fewer substitutes and greater necessity has an inelastic demand – even if prices are raised, people still need to buy it. Obviously you can't sell the real necessities of life – water, air, etc., but you can get the same reduced elasticity of demand by selling a product to a limited demographic. Products aimed at a smaller demographic have fewer suppliers competing so the price isn't driven down to the bare minimum.

Specialization in a niche allows you to become an expert, capable of performing exhaustive research to determine exactly which products best satisfy your demographic, and exactly what information you can draw visitors in with. Becoming an expert on your niche and demographic is key. If you can't effectively capitalize on your niche and please your demographic, than your strategy won't work at all. Members of niche groups are usually more demanding than the general populace. They follow trends, they study minutiae, they have a passion for their particular niche. If you are going to supply these people with products and information, you have develop the same passion. Note that I said develop: if you are already an expert in a niche that's fantastic, but you have to go where the money is. Perhaps you're an avid gardener, you know everything there is to know about growing azaleas, but when you research the gardening market, you find it's already saturated. With a little more research, you may discover that you could make a heap of money selling fly fishing supplies. If you don't know the first thing about fly fishing, who cares? Become an expert anyway. If it would allow me meet my financial goals, I would become an expert in pretty much anything. Except oligochaetology - that's just gross.

Knowledge of your niche is important for myriad reasons: choosing your suppliers and product line, designing your website, interacting with your customers, and above all, adding valuable content to your website. Valuable content is an important part of SEO (Search Engine Optimization), traffic attraction, customer satisfaction, building professionalism and trust, and engaging word-of-mouth referrals and repeat business. Informational content is more crucial on a niche website than on a regular run-of-the-mill site. As I said, niche shoppers are passionate about their interest: they're hungry for information, and they're far more interested in making a personal connection with a retailer, including reading their blog or Tip of the Day and posting questions and comments on message boards.

Now that I've (hopefully) sold you on the idea of entering a niche market, let's talk about choosing your niche. A good place to start is brainstorming hobbies, activities, and interests you're knowledgeable about. Maybe you're a chess champion, an avid scuba diver, or you restore classic cars. Those are all possible niches you could look into. If that doesn't give you any viable leads, then think what your friends and family are interested in.

A second way to brainstorm is to examine your online purchases from the last month or year. This is a useful method because you'll be coming up with products that you know people actually buy online. Also, you'll probably find that most items you buy online naturally come from niche markets. Common, generalized products can be bought at physical locations close to your home. You go online for two reasons: to get the best price, or to purchase quirky, unusual, or specialized items you can't find at the mall. If I were to brainstorm products I've bought online in the last month I would come up with the following ideas: used books, new books, video games, t-shirts, swim trunks, calligraphy sets, jewelry-making supplies, aprons, gift baskets, theater tickets, and boots. On closer examination, I would see that these products are even more specific than I thought – the t-shirt was a funny Hebrew t-shirt which could represent the niche market "funny t-shirts" or "Hebrew/religious items". The swim trunks were Cubs trunks, and more appropriately belong in the "sports memorabilia" category. The apron was a vintage-style Hanne hostess apron, and the boots were studded motorcycle boots.

The products you brainstorm can represent an expanded or contracted niche market. For example, if I focused on the studded motorcycle boots as a possible product to sell online, I could expand that idea to some kind of punk, emo, or gothic website. If I considered the gift baskets, I could contract that to specifically selling baby shower gift baskets. The point of this exercise is to think as prolifically as possible. Once you've got some good ideas, you can narrow down your options by researching the logistics of each possibility.

Now remember, not all products are available for resale online. Immediately I can see that not all my potential products are appropriate for resale, like the theater tickets. You can't sell a product if there's no supplier. Even if there are suppliers for your product line, there may be some restrictions depending on your niche. For instance, I mentioned aprons as a specific segment of the clothing industry you could focus on. One thing you would discover about hostess aprons is that a large percentage of the manufacturers are extremely small operations. They often make and sell their own aprons, and the whole team may consist of one, two, or three people. This means there are few manufacturers capable of dropshipping, and only a few more able to wholesale their product. Hostess aprons are an industry that lacks an extensive manufacturer/distributor/retailer network. If you wanted to enter this niche, you'd have to be flexible.

The second factor to consider is your potential market: do some research to see whether there are already dozens of websites selling the products you had in mind. Also consider exactly how many people are interested in this niche: for something as broad as birdwatching, you can assume you're not the only aficionado, but for a niche like anvil shooting, you may be your only customer. A lot of people advocate performing searches on Google, etc., and analyzing the results to fit into a particular range (not too many hits, not too few). I think you have to look at more than numbers. Your market research should involve a specific and in-depth analysis of the websites already involved in your niche and the potential customers you might attract. An excellent way to examine the latter factor is by scouting out message boards and forums dedicated to your niche. This is something you want to do even after you've chosen a niche – by talking to devotees of your particular niche, you can determine the best products to focus on, and holes in the current supply - products no one is selling, information people are hungry for.

This is really a key point in choosing your market. You have to find a need that's not being filled. People will say, "I want to start a website where people can buy custom-printed items like postage stamps and mugs, just like Zazzle." Well, Zazzle is already doing that, so how are you going to compete with them? You can enter a market that already has suppliers, but you need to find a point of difference, a way to fill a need that the other suppliers aren't filling.

Once you've done your research, if you still have multiple niche markets to choose from, consider making your choice based off a supplier. Chapter 4 covers finding suppliers, and let me say now that it isn't always an easy task. If you find a fantastic dropshipper or wholesaler for one of your niches, that's probably the market you should get started in.

Chapter 3

Time To Brainstorm: Picking Your Product

This chapter could easily be reversed with Chapter 4: Finding a Supplier. In some cases you'll have a definite idea of a product you want to sell, but often your product line will be heavily influenced by what is available from the suppliers in your particular niche market. For this reason, I don't want you to take the "Picking Your Product" title too literally. What we're going to do in this chapter is brainstorm some product ideas, but we're going to flexible. We're going to come up with a number of options, because there may not be a supplier available for the particular product you have in mind, or your product may not sell as well or be as profitable as you expected. You can't be married to your ideas: you need to be liquid, malleable. You need to adapt to circumstances.

Your product line will always be flexible and changeable. Your niche market is not quite as flexible, especially after you've built a website, so you want to make sure you're on the right track when you make that decision. Imagine that you've decided soccer moms are your niche market, and you've decorated your entire website with black and white octagons and minivans, but then you realize soccer moms aren't so great after all and you want to switch to motorcycle gear. You would have to scrap your whole site. However, if you started off selling video cameras and scrapbooks to soccer moms and you decided to switch to day planners and Prozac, that's a much easier switch to make. (Note: You cannot actually dropship Prozac. That was a joke.)

Your product line will probably change all the time. You might want to add holiday products, or bring in a cutting-edge new item. You need to stay current with trends, and you'll want to axe products that aren't selling well. This is a natural state of affairs for an online business, and you shouldn't be afraid to make changes.

So how do you choose a product or multiple products to start out with? If you were successful in selecting a niche market in the previous chapter, then you can simply brainstorm products that represent that niche market. If you couldn't think of a niche, you can skip the chicken and start looking for eggs. There are a few factors to consider when brainstorming product ideas:

Factor #1: Profitability

Your product needs to have the potential to make money. Pick an item too cheap, and your profit margin will be tiny. You'd have to sell a hundred bars of soap to make a substantial profit, or hundreds of sheets of scrapbooking paper (and who would pay $6 to have a 50 cent item shipped to them?). If your product is too expensive, it's much more difficult to sell, and relies more heavily on the image of security your company has cultivated. Thus, while luxury items like diamond jewelry can certainly be sold online, you'll probably want to wait until your business is well-established and positively rated with the BBB, eBay, etc. A good rule of thumb is to begin with products that retail in the $30-150 range, or even more conservatively, in the $40-60 range. These products will be expensive enough to offer a reasonable profit margin, but not so pricey that customers will be leery to purchase them through a small online business.

Profitability depends on more than the sticker price of your product; it also relies on the profit margin of your particular product. Not all products are sold with a generous profit margin; for instance, competition in the electronics market has made the margin quite slim indeed. For this reason, you may not make much money off each sale even if you're selling an $800 LED screen TV. So remember, the most expensive item isn't necessarily the most profitable. The best way to calculate the profitability of a potential product is to make a chart like the one shown below. Be sure to include any costs or fees that might eat into your profit margin.

For simplicity's sake, the following chart lists only potential dropshipping products. As you can see, the most expensive product (the fishing pole) is actually the least profitable. In this chart, the corporate gift baskets would be the best choice (assuming you can sell an equal number of each product listed).

Jeweled Sandals (Retail Price $38):	
Purchase Price of Product:	$18.00
Dropship Fees:	$4
Total Cost:	$22.00
Profit:	$16.00
Corporate Gift Baskets (Retail Price $85):	

Purchase Price of Product:	$50.00
Dropship Fees:	$6
Total Cost:	$56.00
Profit:	$29.00

Fishing Poles (Retail Price $120.00)	
Purchase Price of Product:	$99.00
Dropship Fees:	$7.50
Total Cost:	$106.50
Profit:	$13.50

Factor #2: Availability

You need to consider two kinds of availability: the availability of the product in general to anyone who might want to buy it, and the availability to you for resale. The latter is important because not all products are available for resale. For instance, when brainstorming products most people immediately start to list brand-name products. While many brand-name products are available for resale, most big names are not. Brand-name products almost always have more stringent resale requirements: a large line of credit, massive orders, brick-and-mortar establishments, price controls, exclusivity agreements, etc. This doesn't mean you should discount all brand-names, but you will probably have to forget the super-elite brands like Gucci, Fendi, Coach, Nike, and Apple. As I said before, you can sometimes sell these products from refurbished or overstock suppliers, but in general they can't be used as the basis of a product line. Mid-range brand-names like Wrangler, Saucony, and Capezio are usually more permissive. When brainstorming, I would focus most on products that do not require a recognizable brand to sell, like wedding favors or rain boots.

The availability of the product to the general populace is likewise an important factor because very few people will buy something online that they can purchase at the corner store. When brainstorming product ideas you want to think of products that either are not available to purchase in physical locations close to people's homes, or have a limited selection. For instance, one of the most successful online business entrepreneurs I've worked with sold belt buckles online. Belt buckles can be purchased in the mall, but generally not in any vast or varied selection. Belt buckles were also a good choice because they exemplify Factor #1 (they are right in the $30-60 range), and they perfectly satisfy Factor #3.

Factor #3: Shipping

Cogitate carefully the hassles of shipping the products you're considering. Extremely heavy or unwieldy products are not generally suitable for selling online. I would avoid stainless steel appliances, trampolines, swimming pools, or anything else that requires a crane to move it. Fragile products are likewise not the best idea – if you do want to sell crystal figurines or wine glasses, make sure your dropshipper accepts returns if the item arrives in multiple pieces. Belt buckles are a great example of an easy-to-ship product: small, light, easy to package, near indestructible. Shipping is an important element in product selection because it can take a hefty bite out of your profit margin. Even if you plan to pass the cost of shipping on to your customer, you have to consider what a deterrent hefty shipping fees are. The cost of the item plus shipping has to be comparable to what a customer could purchase the product for elsewhere. In a recent Ernst and Young study of internet sales, shipping costs were cited as the number one concern of 53% of online shoppers, whereas the chance of having their credit card number stolen was only a distant second at 19%.

Now that we've set the guidelines for brainstorming products, let's get to work on the heavy lifting. Really there are thousands of products you can sell online for a profit. I often find that the easiest way to get the juices flowing is to review an example list. This is a list of prospective products I compiled for members who couldn't think of anything to sell online. These are all products I've seen successfully sold online, but I'm not promising success with any of these products. Whether you succeed or fail depends on a number of factors including the particular products you pick from each category, how cheaply you purchase your stock for, how well you market your products, and many other variables.

Product Ideas List:

Action figures

Adult products

African art

Art supplies

Baby products

Baby Boomer products

Bamboo products

BBQ sets and marinades

Beading supplies

Beer-themed products

Belly dancing costumes

Belt buckles

Billiards supplies

Bird feeders/houses

Bonsai products

Breast pumps

Butterfly feeders

Cake decorating supplies and equipment

Camping gear

Chess sets

Children's dress-up clothes (costumes)

Chocolate-dipped fruit

Christian/Religious products

Christmas ornaments and wreaths

Clocks (Grandfather, cuckoo, etc.)

Collegiate sports-themed products

Craft kits

Dance shoes

Darts

Diabetic products

Diecast toys/Models

Doll clothes

Easter/church hats and suits

Eco-friendly/Green products

Egyptian-themed products

Emergency/Survival kits

First-aid kits

Fishing gear

Fitness products

Flags

Fondue sets

Freeze-dried camping/emergenc y food

Gardening products

Geriatric-care products

Gift baskets

Gloves and scarves

Gourmet coffee

Gourmet cookies

Gourmet popcorn

Greek products

Hair accessories

Hemp products

Henna kits

Hiking products

Holiday-themed decorations

Hostess aprons

Hunting gear

Inflatable pool toys

Japanese Anime products

Jewelry

Jewelry-making supplies

Journals

Juggling supplies

Karaoke equipment

Kitchen products

Laptop bags

Left-handed products

Lunchboxes

Luxury sheets/bedding

Mailboxes

Manicure and pedicure supplies

Maps

Martial arts equipment

Masks

Massage oil

Maternity clothing

Mineral makeup

Moccasins

Model trains

Motivational/Inspirational products

Motorcycle apparel

Movie-themed products

Musical instruments

Native American jewelry and belt buckles

Natural cleaning products

Nightlights

Obama products

Period clothing

Plus-size clothing

Poker products

Police/Combat gear

Posters

Products made from a particular material like cedar or stone

Puppets

Puzzles

Rain gear

Reading glasses

Retainer holders (funky fun ones)

RC toys

Robes (bathrobes, kimonos, etc.)

Robotic toys

Rock hunting supplies

Roller derby supplies

Rustic decor

Scales

Science kits

Scouting supplies

Scrubs

Security and nanny cameras

Skateboarding gear

Skincare products

Sorority and fraternity items

Snorkling gear

Solar products

Spa/Relaxation products

Special-needs products

Sports gear

Sports memoribilia

Swords and armor

T-shirts (funny, political, etc.)

Tarot, Astrology, and Palmistry supplies

Tea and tea sets

Theme products (butterfly, fairy, Hawaiian, political, 80s, medieval, etc.)

Tie-dye kits

Toys

Tropical/vacation clothing

Unusual or hand-made board games

Vegan products

Vitamins/supplements

Water bottles

Wedding favors

Weightlifting supplements and protein shakes

Western products

Wind chimes

Wine accessories

Walking sticks and canes

Wallets

You also might consider creating your own product. I don't mean that you should buy a sewing machine and start cranking out baby blankets, because not everybody has the skill set to manufacture a product, and that often isn't the most profitable tactic anyway. What I mean is that you can find a supplier for a general product, say t-shirts, and then work with them to create your own custom product line. For example, I worked with a lady who wanted to sell products for nurses. She wanted to supply the usual items like scrubs and comfy white shoes, but she also wanted to sell cute, sassy nurse-themed t-shirts. I helped her find suppliers for all these products, but unfortunately she didn't like any of the t-shirts the suppliers carried. I told her what she should really do is have her own t-shirts printed. We came up with a bunch of slogans like "Nurses Get The Best Drugs" and "Careful, You Might Be Staring Up At Me From A Table Someday". This tactic ended up being much more beneficial to her because she loved the product and even more importantly, she was offering something that nobody else was selling. No one else had those exact t-shirts because she had created them herself.

Chapter 4

The Hunt Is On: Finding A Supplier

Most people imagine that finding a supplier will be one of the easier parts of setting up their online business. Manufacturers need retailers to sell their products, so how hard could it be right? In actuality, finding a supplier is one of the most crucial and most difficult steps in the process. The reason why finding a supplier is so difficult is because there are many, many middlemen masquerading as legitimate suppliers.

What is a middleman? A middleman is someone who stands between you and the actual manufacturer of the product, taking a bite out of your profit margin. Sometimes this bite is so big you can't make any profit at all, or may actually lose money buying items from them.

Your goal in searching for a supplier is to purchase directly from the manufacturer. This is the best-case scenario: you get the product at the cheapest price direct from the source. Sometimes, buying directly from the manufacturer isn't possible. For instance, bowling ball manufacturers generally sell only to pro-shops, not to retailers. If you want to purchase bowling balls, you usually have to purchase them from a distributor. You may also have to purchase from a distributor if you don't meet the manufacturer's requirements. A few months ago I was searching for a supplier for Lego Star Wars for one of my clients. I called Lego directly, and was told that they would supply Lego Star Wars for resale, but only if the retailer had a website that had been in continuous operation for the last 24 months. My client was still in the process of setting up his website, so obviously he wasn't going to meet this requirement any time soon. However, there was a toy distribution company who supplied Lego Star Wars that he could work with. His profit margin wasn't quite as large, but it was still worth his while.

On the very rare occasion you might decide to purchase from a middleman if you are still able to make a good profit. For instance, some people use middlemen to purchase imported products - they don't want to deal with the hassles of working with an international supplier, so they purchase from a middleman who handles the imports. Since the products are so cheap to begin with, this can still be profitable. But in general you want to avoid middlemen like a Jonas Brothers concert.

The problem is, middlemen aren't always easy to spot. There are a number of companies who offer "thousands of products" to would-be entrepreneurs, or even a "full-service deal" including website hosting. The problem is, they are not the manufacturer of those thousands of products. They're a middleman, probably adding a surcharge on every item, and standing between the retailer and the real supplier so they can't negotiate better prices. Furthermore, these products are the same products that everybody else who works with the company is selling. I've seen people post fifty different items from a company like this on eBay, and not a single one sells. You're out $100 in listing fees, plus whatever you paid for your lifetime membership to the scam supplier. You always get the best deal when you go direct to the source.

So how can you find the right kind of supplier?

1. If you already know a brand-name product you want to sell, sometimes you can contact the manufacturer directly. The only problem with this is the time you spend searching and trying to get hold of somebody.

2. You can perform a Google search to find suppliers by typing "dropship Frisbees" or "wholesale walking sticks". The problem with this route is you will pull up a whole lot of trash and very few treasures. Many of the listings on the first few SERPs (Search Engine Response Pages) will be companies like the ones I mentioned above, or directories, or international suppliers. While you may find a few legitimate suppliers by sifting through all the garbage, you have to keep in mind that these are the same suppliers any other retailer can find by doing a Google search.

3. The best way to find legitimate suppliers is to pay for access to a quality database.

Note that I said *quality* database: anyone can set up a database with a few suppliers in it and start charging for access. Make sure the company you use is reputable and professional. Now obviously I'm going to advocate using the WholesaleRelations.com database, but it's not just because I'm biased. There are a number of reasons why WholesaleRelations.com provides the best access to quality suppliers. First, they have a Research Team who will do all the work for you. The Research Team is composed of experienced professionals who know exactly how to search and are familiar with the best suppliers. You don't have to waste your time because they do all the work for you. If they don't currently have a supplier who fits what you're looking for, they will actually go out and find someone for you - nobody else in the industry does that. The second reason I recommend WholesaleRelations.com is because they offer a 100% money back guarantee. If you don't make the cost of your membership back, they will refund it in full at the end of the year, as long as you have used their services at least once a month (this means you need to call or email or submit a Research Request once a month).

When you've found a number of potential suppliers through a database or online search, the first thing you want to do is check out their website and/or product line. Most suppliers will email you a pdf file with all their products and prices if they're not listed on their website. Once you've decided who you would be interested in working with, you need to contact the dropshipper or wholesaler to set up an account. Some suppliers require you to fill out a credit application or provide identification like a driver's license. Some might want to see your website or receive a copy of your business plan. One thing most legitimate suppliers will require is a Reseller's Permit and/or Tax ID number, so don't try to avoid getting those. The Reseller's Permit allows you to avoid paying tax twice on resale items and the Tax ID number will help you file your taxes at the end of the year.

Before you submit your application, make sure you are familiar with the supplier's policies on dropship fees, shipping methods, returns, refunds, customer support, blind dropshipping, payment requirements, and any other questions you might have.

Your supplier will usually stipulate whether they prefer to be contacted via phone or email. Email is the common medium for most business transactions, but I would recommend making at least one or two phone calls as well. Speaking to a supplier representative is an important part of building a relationship. Above all, make sure you are always courteous and well-prepared when you contact a supplier: have your questions ready and your purpose in mind. Never, never behave in an overly casual or demanding manner with your supplier. These may seem like elementary mandates, but I can't tell you how often I receive business emails with poor spelling / punctuation / grammar, profanity, and inappropriate quotes under the signature. No supplier is obligated to work with you, and they won't if you don't impress them. Building a relationship with your supplier is a process: you have to prove your professionalism and dedication. After you've sold a respectable volume of product, you can negotiate for perks like lower dropshipping fees, better shipping rates, bulk discounts, etc., but don't try to do this right away - first you need to prove that your partnership is beneficial to their business.

In passing I've mentioned using an international supplier. By "international", I mean a dropshipper or wholesaler not located in your country. If you don't live in the United States, you may be forced to use an international supplier, depending on the product you're trying to sell and the method you wish to utilize. Canada, the UK, and Australia are in the process of developing their own dropshipping supply chain, so there are more drosphippers available in these countries than in some others, but they don't yet have the selection the US does. People located outside the US can still dropship-retail, but they may need to be more flexible. (For more details on this, see chapter 13).

Let's assume that you live in the US. You might be tempted to use an international supplier so you can purchase cheap Asian manufactures or indigenous products from Africa, India, Egypt, etc. Using an international supplier offers a certain amount of exclusivity: you can often obtain products that are not currently being sold in the US, or are sold by few other retailers. Additionally, most Asian-based dropshippers are extremely anxious to build relationships with US-based sellers, in contrast to some persnickety domestic suppliers.

I'm not against using an international supplier: I've seen plenty of people make money doing it. However, it can be much more risky than using a domestic supplier. You have to deal with language barriers, customs hassles, expensive/slow shipping, payment issues, and problems with quality and returns. It's very difficult to tell ahead of time how sophisticated and reliable a foreign company is. Purchasing wholesale can alleviate some of your issues: the speed of shipping isn't a factor since the product is shipped from you to the customer, instead of direct from China, and this likewise allows you to check quality before the product is sent out. However, the rest of your issues remain in full force.

If you do decide to purchase from an international supplier, particularly an Asian one, make sure you cross your Ts and dot your Is in the following areas:

1. Strenuously research international suppliers before you work with them. Major Asian suppliers are reviewed on sites like www.dropshipforum.co.uk and www.rateitall.com. On these sites you can read the experiences of other retailers who have worked with your prospective supplier. You can also scan the message boards for examples of potential issues you might run up against when using a supplier from a particular foreign country.

2. Find out if there are any fees associated with your potential supplier's service (order fees, monthly fees, etc.), and whether there is a minimum quantity of products you have to buy in order to get the best price. When you contact an international supplier, have a list of questions ready and make sure you get them all answered; it's easy to get off track and neglect to have all questions answered fully when you're dealing with a linguistic or cultural disconnect.

3. Determine which promotional materials will be furnished. The product descriptions may not be in English and will almost certainly need to be tailored to your purposes, but at the very least you need photos of every product you are planning to sell. Also, make sure the supplier updates their catalog regularly so you're not selling items they don't actually have – they should email you if they run out of stock on anything.

4. If you're dropship-retailing, you need to ensure that the quality of the product will be consistent. Your dropshipper should be willing to send you a sample of the product. You should also ask about their quality-control regulations, which should be in place both at the factory level and again at the supplier's warehouse. Your products should come with an extensive guarantee (a 1 year warrantee is common). Some products will have to be purchased wholesale so you can monitor the quality yourself. One of my associates makes a lot of money buying fake Juicy tracksuits and knock-off designer jeans from an Asian company and re-selling them on eBay (she doesn't sell them as genuine of course). She buys 5-10 items of

clothing at a time and has them shipped to her house. The items are excellent imitations, but the sizes vary drastically: she'll buy two Smalls, and one will be tiny and the other quite large. This isn't a problem for her, because she simply posts them as Small and Large on eBay, but it would definitely be an issue if you dropshipped the item directly to your customer.

5. Customs are a much bigger issue when dropship-retailing. Your customers will be very upset if their orders are hung up for weeks or never arrive at all. Look for suppliers who offer expedited next-day processing, and ensure your supplier uses reliable services like UPS, FedEx, etc. Even so, packages from China usually take 10 days or longer to arrive, so make sure your eBay listings or website clearly indicates the expected arrival date.

6. Some customers are annoyed when they purchase from an American company and the product arrives from Asia. Many international suppliers provide blind dropshipping, but you have to check with the company to determine exactly what this entails (for instance, sometimes a packing slip is still included). If you think blind dropshipping is a necessity for your business, ensure that packages will be sent in plain, non-identifiable packaging and will not contain any receipts or packing materials that give away the real source of the product.

7. Paying your International/Asian supplier can be difficult. Credit cards are under government restriction in China and some of the common payment systems like Western

Union and wire transfers are untraceable. Make sure any funds you send overseas are sent through verifiable sources. An escrow payment service is your best option: you deposit the funds, which the supplier can see but not access. The supplier ships the goods to your customer, and can only access the funds after the package arrives. If you do set up an account for wire transfers, make sure this account is only used to pay your international supplier and does not have any other funds in it.

When researching products from Asia, you should be aware that 99% of brand-name products are knock-offs, whether the company acknowledges it or not. Some are made to look exactly like the real thing, while others are sold as unbranded alternatives- a phone that looks very much like an iPhone, for instance. There is definitely a market for this kind of product, or you can sell cheap, generic items where brand isn't an issue.

Some common products dropshipped from Asia include:

Computers, computer components, cell phones, mp3 players, lingerie, clothing, jewelry, watches, handbags, shoes, pet products, and electronics accessories of all kinds.

The final thing I want to talk about in this chapter is the decision whether to use a single supplier or multiple suppliers. Many people setting up an online business would prefer to use a single dropshipper or wholesaler to supply all their products. Using a single supplier is convenient because it simplifies your business operations: whenever a product is sold on your website or on eBay, you know exactly where you need to get it from. Presumably, you are also choosing a dropshipper who you trust, who you can rely on; this takes some of the stress out of your life. However, there are benefits to using more than one dropshipper.

The first benefit is increased selection. While some dropship suppliers offer a wide range of products, the best ones usually do not. That's because the best dropshippers are usually the manufacturers or direct distributors of a certain product, like rug-hooking kits or cowboy boots. They don't also supply pet products and hunting gear and kitchen sinks. Sometimes it's totally fine to have a website that only sells one product, like posters, but you might want to supplement your product line with other items that mesh well with your original product (say, movie memorabilia). In that case, you might need additional suppliers.

The second benefit is reliable supply. Should something go wrong with your first supplier, say, they run out of stock on certain items, or worse, close up shop, you don't want your entire online business to be crippled. Using multiple suppliers means you're not dependent on one partner.

The third benefit involves experimentation and competition. If you only ever use one dropshipper or wholesaler, how will you know you're getting the best deal on your products? If you have a couple of suppliers for the same product line, you might be pleasantly surprised when one offers you a bigger bulk discount or a bonus for sales volumes.

I'm not saying you should get a dozen different suppliers, because that would make your business operations complicated, but it's a good idea to build your business around two or three really solid suppliers. Once you are comfortable with your current suppliers, you can certainly branch out and add a few more. In terms of selection, supply, experimentation, and competition, it's beneficial to your online business to diversify your supply chain.

Chapter 5

A Room Of Your Own: Picking Your Sales Venue

Now that you have a product and a supplier for that product, what you need is somewhere to sell. There are a multitude of places you can sell products online: Bonanzle, Etsy, Craigslist, Amazon, and a hundred other sites, but the most common venues for online business entrepreneurs are eBay and a personal website. Those are the two options we're going to discuss now, though we'll talk about the others in later chapters.

First: Selling on eBay.

It's very easy to set up an eBay and PayPal account and start posting items. It's somewhat harder to actually make profitable sales. Chapter 6 will be devoted exclusively to selling on eBay: how to format your listings, how to write a great product description, when to open an eBay store, and so on and so forth. For now all I'll say is eBay is a great place to get your feet wet. It's a place where you can accustom yourself to online sales, test which products sell well, and try out a prospective dropshipper or wholesaler's services.

The one thing you need to be very careful of on eBay is keeping your customer rating high. Every time you sell a product on eBay your buyer has the opportunity to rate you. This rating is very important because subsequent buyers check to see how reliable you are, and you need a high rating to access certain features on eBay like your own eBay store. On occasion keeping your rating high might require you to lose money on a sale. For instance, a buyer may want to return an item for a stupid reason, or you may make a mistake when posting a price and have to sell the product for a loss. It's better to take a small loss one time than to torch your rating, because no amount of money can buy that rating back. Even if you think you won't sell on eBay for very long, protect your rating like it's your infant: you don't know when you may need it in the future.

Second: Selling from a personal website.

Chapter 7 will offer an in-depth analysis of how to sell from your own website including website design tips, choosing a host and domain name, and an overview of SEO (Search Engine Optimization). For now, suffice it to say that setting up a website is going to require an investment of time and money. Don't start on your website until you have a pretty solid idea of which products you're going to sell, who's going to supply you, and who you're going to market to. The last thing you want is to have to scrap your website and start over because you're not actually going to be able to sell Mariah Carey-themed products or Cuban cigars. Your website also takes longer to get rolling: it will take time to improve your search engine ranking and start bringing in traffic. You might not make money off your site right away. For this reason, and for the aforementioned practice, you might want to start selling on eBay and then transition into running your own website.

You don't necessarily need to choose between selling on eBay and operating a website. Many online retailers do both. In fact, you can use your eBay listings to drive traffic to your website. While you're not really allowed to actively promote your website in your eBay listings, there are a few ways you can get around the restrictions:

First, you can put a link to your website on your eBay account in the About Me section. Many people who browse your listing will click on the link and come to your website. Also, the inbound link will help your website's search engine ranking.

Second, you can invite your eBay customers to visit your website through emails or newsletters. You don't want to be obnoxious about this, but good customer service can include sending a thank-you email to your customer when a deal closes on eBay. It's not out of place to say "Thank you for choosing Sunshine Industries for your stationary needs! We appreciate your business! Please visit us again at www.SunshineIndustries.com."

The effectiveness of promoting your website on eBay depends in large part on how many sales you make and how much your customers like you. While the results probably won't justify using this as your only marketing technique, it's an example of how eBay sales and website sales can be symbiotic.

Ultimately, I would recommend starting out with eBay sales. EBay can be a classroom where you accustom yourself to online business, where you can test and prepare before expanding your operations. Once you have a certain amount of eBay experience, you can graduate to an eBay store or to operating your own website (we'll talk more about eBay stores in Chapter 6). Even after you have a website up and running, there's no reason why you shouldn't continue selling on eBay, particularly around holidays. eBay is great place to sell products that you've purchased a limited supply of, say in one-time clearance deals. Many people purchase products for ridiculous prices on Black Friday, then sell them on eBay in the following weeks for a hefty profit. These kinds of sales are more appropriate for eBay than for a website where you would want to carry a regular supply of a specific product line.

Chapter 6

Start the Auction: Selling Products on eBay

The ease of posting an item on eBay might tempt you to start clicking away like a madman, but if you want to run a profitable operation you need to learn the eBay universe. A huge amount of sales are made on eBay every day, but competition can be steep, particularly in categories like electronics. Thus, as in all aspects of online business, you need to bring your A-Game. The first thing you want to do is learn the eBay terminology: you need to know what terms like "Buy It Now", "Auction-style listing", and "Reserve Price" mean - there is a glossary at the end of this book that will be helpful in this regard. You also need to familiarize yourself with eBay's rules and regulations so you don't accidentally get penalized or banned. Finally, you can check out the educational articles in eBay's "How to Sell" and "News and Updates" sections, and monitor the "Seller Central and "What's Hot" sections of eBay for popular product and seller updates. Once you're familiar with the eBay process, you can proceed to the steps for listing a product.

Step #1: Research

When you have a potential product you want to sell on eBay, you have to research to see if you will be able to sell it for a profit. One of the best ways to do this is to perform an Advanced Search. By clicking on the Advanced Search button, you can search only completed listings (listings that have actually sold). Search for completed listings similar to the item you want to sell. By averaging the price similar items have sold for, you can get a good idea of your expected sale price. You can also check out the listings that sold for the highest amount and see what those sellers did right (how they formatted their listing, which keywords they used, how many pictures/videos they added, etc.) When performing a search of completed listings, make sure the listings you are examining are actually comparable to your product: it's easy to overlook whether the item was used/new/refurbished, came with free shipping, and so on and so forth.

Step #2: Formatting Your Listing

Once you have a product you're fairly certain will sell for a good price on eBay, you need to post a listing. There's an art to composing a great eBay listing. A great listing is easy for buyers to find and effectively pitches the product. To make it easy to find, you need to post to the right category with a snappy title. The title should describe the product and include searchable keywords, while remaining as short as possible. For example, here's the title of a product off the Daily Deals on www.wholesalerelations.com: "Red Garnet and Honey Citrine Journey Pendant Necklace in 10 K Gold". This is a pretty good title: It includes keywords like garnet, pendant necklace, and gold. It also includes attractive adjectives like "honey citrine" instead of just "citrine", and states the brand name "Journey". I might have made it a little shorter: "Journey Pendant Necklace in Garnet, Honey Citrine, and Gold ". Garnet is usually some shade of red, so I wouldn't bother to mention its color in the title unless it was one of the more unusual black, brown, or purple shades. Also, 10 K gold isn't as impressive as 18 or 24 K gold, so I would put that in the body of the product description, not the title.

Along with the title, you need a solid product description. Your product description should clearly and concisely describe the product, highlighting all selling features. Remember, most product descriptions cannot be copied verbatim from other sources. Even if you're granted the rights by your dropshipper or wholesaler, you'll probably want to tweak the description. A great product description should include the following:

A. **Specific Marketing:** Know who your intended market is before you begin writing your product description. If you're marketing to teenage girls, your tone would be quite different than a pitch aimed at 50-year old businessmen. The rare product can be marketed to almost anyone (e.g. cell phones), but usually you'll have a buyer in mind. You don't want to be too extreme with targeting, because you may catch other demographics in your net. If you're selling glitter lip-gloss, you don't necessarily want to say, "'Sup girls, want 2 look hot at prom?" because there may be other people interested in your lipgloss who would be turned off by this tone. Subtle angling should suffice.

B. **Keywords:** Searchable keywords should be sprinkled in the title and body of your product description. A keyword is a word you would type into a search box when looking for a product. For instance, if I wanted designer dog clothing, I might type in the keywords "dog clothing", "designer dog clothing", "doggie bling", "fancy dog clothes", etc. When adding keywords to your listing, don't keyword-stuff (don't throw in every word you can possibly think of). Make sure your description remains concise, exciting, and relevant.

C. **Photos:** A picture is worth a thousand sales. The more attractive the photo, the more sales. It's important for the photo to show the entire product, and if a portion of the product has fine detail, an additional close-up shot can display this. Photos from all sides are often used on eBay (360 degree view), and another object can be used to show the scale of the product. For instance, on Etsy jewelry is often posed with common household items, like a pair of earrings dangling from a pencil. Everyone knows how large a pencil is, so the scale of the earrings is immediately apparent. Just make sure it doesn't appear that the two items are being sold together, like a set of speakers next to a TV.

D. **Brand:** If the product has a recognizable brand-name, the name should feature prominently in the description. For products like electronics the brand should always be disclosed, but for other items like jewelry or clothing, it's not necessary if it doesn't help the sale. If I told you my shirt was from "Suzy Shier" that probably wouldn't mean anything to you – it's not relevant unless it's a recognizable brand-name like Calvin Klein, Ed Hardy, Roxy, etc.

E. **Size and Measurements:** It's not enough to show the size of the item in the photo, it should also be clearly indicated in your product description. This is not important for standard-size items like books or DVD players, but is very important for home décor items, TVs, clothing, etc.

F. **Colors and Patterns:** For clarity's sake and also to enhance your description, a verbal explanation of colors and patterns is often useful. A computer screen may not show the exact shade of a blue dress; adjectives like "royal blue", "sky blue", or "turquoise blue" not only clarify the color, but aid in the attractive and desirable image you are building with your words. Make sure you understand what "royal blue" means, though: if the dress shows up and it's actually pastel, it may be returned.

G. **Small Details:** Again, you want to describe your product as accurately as possible and also make it sound attractive. Describing the small details of the product like "anti-shock capability", "distressed finish", and "antique pearl buttons" make the product more real for the customer, building an image of solidity and value. It also helps ensure that your customer won't be unpleasantly surprised when the product arrives.

H. **Uses and Features:** Research your product before writing your description. Besides including all the basic features like "Surround speakers and subwoofer", include suggestions for use like "can be easily installed in any size car" or "a necessary component of any home theater system". Don't be cheesy about this: while researching this chapter I found use suggestions like "wow your friends with this sleek and stylish attaché case". The phrase "wow your friends" only worked on twelve-year old boys buying x-ray glasses off the back page of Reader's Digest in 1952. You don't want to come off like a snake-oil salesman.

I. **Price:** Your price should always be clearly and prominently indicated.

J. **Call To Action:** End your product description with a call to action: "Buy It Now Price: $19.95", or "Free shipping for Memorial Day weekend only". You want to motivate people to buy immediately whenever possible. You can also use up-sell offers as a call to action: "Buy these Victoria's Secret silk pajamas now and get the fluffy bunny slippers $10 off".

When composing your product description, try to focus on why someone would purchase your product over all the others in the same category. This is known as your product's "point of difference". Let's say you're selling wedding dresses on eBay. There are generally two reasons women buy their wedding dress on eBay: to get a smokin' deal, or because they want a hard-to-find style. If you're selling regular wedding dresses, you might want to focus on the great price you're offering and features like free shipping. If you have another point of difference, like "modest wedding dresses", you don't have to base your promotion around price because that's not the main factor for your demographic. Instead, point out how your dresses are perfect for the stylish LDS, Orthodox Jewish, or Islamic bride.

Never post a bunch of identical listings at the same time. If you list three identical plasma-screen TVs, you drive down the value down for all three. Stagger your auctions so you attract different bidders. This is easy to do because you don't actually need a long auction for most items: you might think that the longer you post an item for, the more bids you'll get, but in actuality most bids come in the last 24 hours. You can test the effectiveness of different periods, or use a tool like AuctionBurner.com to predict your best auction duration. For most products, you'll need 3 days or less to get the price bid up.

Never misrepresent your product. Putting irrelevant keywords in your title or product description is keyword-spamming and it really ticks people off. If they actually purchase the item before realizing it isn't what they were looking for, that's even worse because they'll slap you with a chargeback and a negative customer rating.

Step #3: Upselling

One of the best ways to increase your sales volume and profit margin is to up-sell. Up-selling is the process of convincing a customer to purchase one or more products in addition to the one they were initially interested in. Up-selling is a little trickier on eBay than it is on a personal website since you can't add pop-up boxes offering complimentary products or additional offers during the shopping-cart check-out.

There are two basic ways to up-sell on eBay: first, you can send an additional offer along with the invoice or response for the first. For example, when a buyer wins the auction for your camcorder, you can send them an email asking if they would like the camera bag included for one low price of $212, or you could include a coupon offer in their packing materials.

The second way to up-sell is to combine your products into packages or sets in a single listing. For instance, you could post the camcorder and camera bag together as one item with one price, even though they're really two separate items. Not only does this help you to sell two items instead of one, but it helps obscure the prices of individual items so your prices can't be compared as easily. Packages like this are convenient for people who don't have the time or expertise to buy each item individually, like when shopping for gifts or embarking on a new hobby. You could make a whole filmographer starter kit with batteries, a tripod, camcorder, bag, and instructional book, effectively creating a unique product all your own.

Step #4: Customer Communication

Communicating with potential customers is always important, but it is particularly so on eBay where the buyer has no website to judge you from. Your listings and customer satisfaction rating are slim exemplars of your reliability and professionalism, so prospective buyers may have a number of questions before they purchase from you. The most important thing in eBay communication is to be available: you should be checking and responding to emails multiple times a day. To ensure these emails are received and sent properly, turn off your spam filter or lower its settings so customer emails aren't kicked over to your junk folder. Likewise, use the eBay "Contact Member" form to send your emails so you can be sure they're reaching their destination. Lost emails are one of the primary causes of dropped bids and customer dissatisfaction, so I really can't stress this enough. Even after the sale is made, make sure you continue to answer any questions, concerns, or comments your buyer might have. This will help you achieve a high satisfaction rating and repeat business.

One caveat with eBay communication: some scammers pose as potential customers to eke personal information out of you, like your email address or banking information. Don't give away unnecessary information and always communicate through your eBay account, not your personal email or phone line.

Step #5: Payment

No matter what venue you're selling from, you need a method to accept payment from your customers. Cheques and money orders are cumbersome and unreliable, and most customers don't want to pay that way. Your main options for online business transactions are a merchant account and PayPal. A merchant account allows you to process credit card payments. PayPal allows you to take payments from any customer who has a PayPal account. Your customer's PayPal account can include funds from credit cards, debit, bank accounts, sales they've made online, etc. Both a merchant account and PayPal will cost you money and come with certain restrictions.

Merchant accounts can be expensive to set up and usually charge a monthly fee. Some have restrictions which may limit the amount of transactions you can run each month or the total dollar amount you can process. (Often these restrictions are removed after a few months when you've proved your reliability). Merchant accounts are generally more expensive than PayPal to begin with, but depending on your sales volume they may be cheaper in the long run.

PayPal is an extremely popular payment system. Most online shoppers have PayPal accounts, but not everybody. (Your customers must have PayPal accounts to purchase from you unless you use the Virtual Terminal feature for a fee of $30 per month.) Anyone can set up a PayPal account for free, and it doesn't cost your customer anything to buy a product through PayPal, but you will be charged fees every time you make a sale. PayPal fees are usually 1.9-2.9 percent of every sale, plus a 30 cent fee for each transaction. PayPal comes with a Seller Protection Policy, but only if you ship a physical/tangible product or service within seven days to an eligible address with proof of delivery. If you did use PayPal exclusively, it would be easy to monitor and examine your payment data.

The dangerous thing about using PayPal as your only payment option is that PayPal reserves the right to freeze your funds or suspend/cancel your account. On a moment's notice you could be unable to accept payments or access your funds for months at a time, which could shut down your business entirely. These penalties can occur for reasons as obscure as "suspicious activity on the account" i.e. if your sales tripled in one month or you had too many chargebacks. For this reason, I would not recommend using a single payment system, PayPal or a merchant account. That is the very definition of putting all your eggs in one basket, and makes your online business vulnerable to financial stranglehold. Even without the fear of losing your payment processing/fund accessing privileges, it is better to have multiple payment options so you never lose sales.

If you are unable to get a merchant account initially, you can skate by on PayPal for a while, but I would recommend offering your customers both options as soon as possible.

Step #6: Using Tools and Apps to Expand Your Operations

The amount of tools and applications available to boost your eBay sales is roughly equivalent to the amount of beauty aids marketed to women: practically infinite. The purpose of the apps is to reduce your workload and improve your customer's experience, but many of the tools are used for advanced business operations, so you probably won't graduate to using them until you've become much more familiar with eBay sales. Most eBay apps are offered by third-party providers, but can be accessed in the "Selling Manager" section of eBay. Some applications are free while others have a small monthly or annual fee. Before you spend time or money on any of them, make sure they will actually be beneficial to your eBay business and that you are far enough along to use them (some will only be beneficial to those with eBay stores or a high sales volume). The following is a short overview of the major tools and applications (for a more detailed account, visit eBay's SM Apps Directory Page):

A. **123show** – One of the media applications. Allows for enhanced product viewing, like a 360 degree spin.

B. **ah!TEXT Mobile Messenger** – This app sends text message notification every time your eBay account receives customer feedback or a question, offer, or sale. You can customize it so you don't receive every single notification – maybe you want only notification for sales, or sales above a certain dollar amount.

C. **Auctane Shipping Manager** – Allows you to print packing slips and shipping labels for almost any kind of package. You can customize delivery confirmation, signature requirements, etc. Provides you with discounts on some kinds of shipping.

D. **eZ labelZ** – Another app for printing shipping labels, flyers, cards, etc.

E. **ezSupport** – Archives customer correspondence and provides searchable FAQs and auto-response messaging. I would caution against using auto-response emails: canned answers are extremely obnoxious. They rarely address the subtleties of the question asked, which makes their generic nature obvious. There is nothing more annoying than waiting for an email response and then finding the person clearly didn't even read what you wrote – it's disrespectful and not helpful to the customer.

F. **Froo! Template Themes** – A library of ad templates to save time composing a custom ad for each eBay posting. These templates are attractive and professional-looking, so if you struggle with creating effective posts, this may be the app for you.

G. **Link to UPS WorldShip** – Allows you to ship your items through UPS with rekeying order details.

H. **My.ShipRush Ship Center** –Allows you to organize all your shipping from one location even if you are selling from multiple venues (eBay, a website, Amazon, etc.).

I. **MyStoreMaps** - Allows you to download your sales history and current sales to create a map so customers can see where you've shipped products in the past. This is supposed to demonstrate international sales and shipping experience, but obviously is only helpful if you have that kind of experience. If you don't, it won't increase your potential customer's confidence at all, and may in fact backfire, decreasing sales.

J. **MyStoreRewards** – Allows you to create a customizable rewards program for your customers. Includes options such as putting a cap on the amount of rewards that can be earned. Excellent for increasing repeat sales and boosting customer satisfaction ratings.

K. **OrderCup Shipping** – Another app for printing shipping labels, packing slips, invoices, etc. Also sends tracking notices to buyers, combines multiple orders to save on shipping, and so on and so forth.

L. **Outright** – Free online bookkeeping. Track sales and expenses, estimates the taxes you should be paying, keeps track of business write-offs, etc.

M. **Quantity Manager** – Allows you to maintain the image of scarcity in your product listings. This is a common listing technique – you may have hundreds of Tag watches in stock, but you list only three, then two, then one, then none for a day or two, before pretending you got three more in stock. This functions as a "call to action" to prompt people to purchase right away. The app will automatically list stock levels at your predetermined amount. (I find this technique a little sleazy, but it's common in retail, especially for high-end/rare items). Quantity Manager will also warn you when inventory levels are legitimately low.

N. **Review Gadget** – Automatically collects and displays product reviews on your listing page. Also gathers more detailed and specific customer feedback. This is important because, statistically speaking, positive customer feedback provides not only more sales, but sales of a higher dollar amount, and much more repeat business.

O. **Terapeak** –Provides quality market research and data analytics to help you to choose which products to sell and when.

P. **vzaar** – Another media app – this one allows quick and easy addition of video to your listings.

Another eBay tool I mentioned earlier is AuctionBurner.com. This is not a tool available in the Selling Manager section, but rather is a paid service. AuctionBurner.com allows you to plug in a specific product, say a vintage cashmere sweater, and it provides you with a number of selling suggestions. AuctionBurner.com can tell you what the best days are to sell vintage cashmere sweaters, and even the best time of the day to post the listing. It can tell you which keywords you should include in your posting, what the optimum list format is (Auction-Style, Buy It Now, etc.), and how long your auction duration should be. It can even tell you the appropriate category to post your item in and which listing upgrades you should use. You can tailor your search using the Advanced Options and examine the charts generating your results. AuctionBurner.com is useful tool for people just starting out with eBay.   It's available for a small annual membership fee at www.auctionburner.com.

Now that we've reviewed the steps for selling an item on eBay, I'd like to talk about a few more aspects of eBay sales.   First, building your rating. Selling on eBay is kind of a catch-22: it's hard to make sales when you don't have a customer rating, but you can't get a customer rating without making sales. When you first start out, you should probably sell a few cheap items that people won't be afraid to buy from a newbie seller. For instance, you could look around your house and see if there are any items you'd like to sell on eBay just to practice, like that old Lakers jersey you never wear since you moved to Colorado, or the baby clothes your 22 year old son grew out of a long time ago. Making a few sales like this will help you gain experience and build your rating. You can also improve your rating by purchasing items on eBay: instead of heading up to Wal-mart for a new printer cartridge, pick it up on eBay. Finally, you can add ID Verify on your eBay account to enhance your image of security.

Second, let's talk about graduating to an eBay store. When you first start selling on eBay, you'll list single items using the Auction Format. Once you're comfortable with the selling process and your satisfaction rating and sales volume begin to increase, you may consider opening your own eBay store. How do you know when you're ready to make this switch, and what benefits does an eBay store offer?

When are you ready to graduate to an eBay store?

The answer is different for everyone, but basically you're ready when you've gotten a minimum feedback rating of 20 (eBay's rule), and you're prepared to handle multiple active listings at once. Because there's a monthly subscription fee to run your eBay store, you want to make sure your sales volume justifies the expense. You will also have to be verified with eBay (have a valid credit card on file), or have a PayPal account in good standing.

What are the benefits of an eBay store?

First, you have much greater control. You can decorate your store and promote its address. You can fill it with a variety of items, giving you a much greater chance of multiple-item high-volume sales. You can start offering promotions like free shipping on orders over a certain amount, and you can use the tools and apps to track your sales and revenue and promote your products. In your store, you can list numerous items for longer period of time than with traditional listings. You can also build a brand and a name for yourself, something that is much more difficult to do when you are selling via single auction listings. Finally, you can list your items in store inventory format for a much cheaper fee than auction and fixed-price posts.

How do you set up your store?

Once you click on the "Subscribe to Stores" button, the process is quite simple; you won't need to be an expert in web design as you will simply be customizing a template. Any active listings you are currently selling on eBay will automatically appear in your store. The most difficult part may be deciding what level of store to open. There are three subscription levels, so research each one before deciding which level will best fit your needs:

- **Basic Level ($15.95/month):** You may be ready for level one when you are selling 12-50 items per month. You will receive 5 customizable store pages, an email account, customer support during business hours, and eBay tools including Markdown Manager and Selling Manager.

- **Premium Level ($49.95/month):** This level is probably sufficient if you are selling 50-400 items per month. You receive 10 customizable pages, promotion on eBay Stores' homepage, 24 hour customer service, and eBay tools including Selling Manager Pro.

- **Anchor Level ($300/month):** You will probably need this level when you are in the 500+ sales per month range. You receive 15 customizable pages and a better promo on the eBay Stores homepage.

What are the negatives of an eBay store?

If you don't have the sales volume to pay for the store, you're just wasting money. Also, if you put all your items in store inventory format to lessen your eBay fees, they won't be as visible in general searches (by listing your store items in a variety of ways, you can overcome the visibility issues somewhat). Ebay stores have their own rules, so make sure you read the "Rules For Sellers" page on eBay before you begin so you aren't penalized for accidental wrong-doing. Ebay stores are much more complicated than posting and selling a few random items, so make sure you don't take this step before you're ready.

Now I want to talk briefly about selling used/garage sale items on eBay. Obviously, the majority of your product line will probably be new products purchased from a wholesaler or dropshipper, however depending on your niche, you might want to sell a mix of new, used, dropship, wholesale, and randomly acquired items.

To illustrate, let's return to the aforementioned vintage cashmere sweater set. Cashmere is a huge seller on eBay – the most searched-for item in fact. Cashmere holds its value practically forever. It's a premium fabric with a high demand globally and limited supply in many locales. The great thing about cashmere is that it retains value at almost every stage of its life: you could buy a batch of cashmere sweaters, scarves, or gloves wholesale and sell them individually on eBay. You could pick up used cashmere items at yard sales, bazaars, and thrift stores, repairing small holes in the material or having them refurbished to make an even greater profit. You could even sell cashmere in a state of total disrepair to people who use cashmere scraps in craft projects, knitting, sewing, etc. If you were to scour the thrift stores and chance upon an original cashmere twin-set from the 1950s, you would be astounded at what you could sell it for. So if you want to become a major cashmere player on the eBay market, you might consider selling new, used, scrap, and even antique cashmere to capitalize on a variety of demographics.

Part of why I would never expect you to make your whole income off used items is because it requires a huge amount of scouting. You'd have to spend every weekend at church socials and garage sales, and weekdays picking through the racks at Goodwill. But if you have one or two days a week to do a little searching, you can supplement your dropship or wholesale items and expand your customer base.

If you decide to go this route, you can get the best deals second-hand by doing the following:

A. Shop in rich areas. Garage sales in upper-crust neighborhoods are a goldmine for eBay top-sellers like ostrich-skin boots, Vera Wang dresses, leather belts/briefcases/purses, china, scented candles, and premium perfumes and colognes (it's okay if the candles are slightly burned or the perfume bottle is only ¾ full, you can still sell them on eBay).

B. Shop the biggest events. You'll waste time driving around little single-family garage sales. Your best bet is to hit bigger bazaars and fundraisers where you'll find items from dozens or hundreds of different homes and sometimes brand-new items donated by businesses. Look on community websites or Craigslist to find notification of these events.

C. Arrive early. You're not going to be the only professional yard-saler in town, and the best stuff gets snatched up at the beginning of the day.

D. Bring cash and bargain. Most people want to get rid of their unwanted goods and receive a little money in return – they're not picky about the exact cash return. Bargaining is a necessity at every step of the game, and works especially well at the end of the day when sellers want to get rid of whatever is left. Having a small amount of cash visible in your hand while you bargain is a good technique: it's like holding a chocolate bar while you tell a kid to go clean their room. Offering to purchase a whole box of items like cosmetics or books for one price is also a good way to get a deal.

E. **Always, always remember shipping.** When selling on eBay, you have to balance the expected sale price against the cost of shipping. People buy on eBay to get a deal or to find rare and unusual items: if your product falls in the former category, shipping better be cheap. If it falls in the latter, you have a little more leeway.

The following are second-hand products that sell well on eBay and are well-suited to round out your dropship /wholesale products:

- Designer clothing
- Designer perfume/cologne
- China (plates, dolls, etc.)
- Leather (coats, motorcycle jackets, purses, briefcases, belts)
- Children's items (sleeping bags, clothing, bedding)
- Cowboy boots (the more out-there the better, including lizard, ostrich, bright colors, embroidered, etc.)
- Sports equipment
- Wedding dresses (contemporary/stylish ones, not nasty sparkly 80s dresses)
- Brand-name kitchen items
- Brand-name cosmetics (better if unopened)
- Gift items (candles, lotion sets, etc, also better if unopened)
- Pretty much anything still in the box/with tags on
- Anything with vintage characters (lunchboxes, t-shirts, bedding, posters, action figures with Super heroes, Charlie Brown, Smurfs, Sesame Street, My Little Pony, etc)

The more vintage/specialty you can get, or the more expensive/designer the better. This means you need to do some research on which quirky 70s items are the most popular and whether Guess or Prada purses are more desirable. As far as antiques go, the minutiae of particular years, makers, types of restoration, states of damage, and so on and so forth are far beyond me. You would have to watch about a thousand hours of Antiques Roadshow before you'd be ready to find authentic Shaker chairs. That's why I recommend vintage over antique – it's more straight-forward, though you do have to watch out for faux-vintage items pumped out by companies like Old Navy.

Unless you really, really enjoy this kind of shopping, I wouldn't recommend used items as your primary product offering, but I do think this is a great way to supplement dropship/ wholesale niche products. It's also another way to build your customer satisfaction rating and get eBay experience.

One final note regarding selling products on eBay: you have to decide whether you will be shipping to international or only domestic locations. Shipping internationally is a little more complicated since you'll have to fill out customs forms and adjust your shipping fees. International buyers also represent a greater fraud threat than domestic buyers.

The determinant of whether you sell domestically or internationally may be your product. Let's go back to cashmere: up to 80% of cashmere items sold on eBay are sold to international buyers. This is because cashmere is not as readily available in other countries as it is in the US. A lot of items can be sold on eBay precisely because they're not easily obtained outside the US or because they're more popular outside the US. Find out if any of your products fall in this category, because you could be missing out on a huge percentage of your sales otherwise.

If you do decide to sell to international buyers, try listing shipping prices to multiple destinations in your eBay post. To protect yourself from fraud, be selective. If an email seems fishy (if it asks for strange information, is far too long and detailed, or seems like a form letter), don't risk the sale. Also, don't assume you're protected because you're using PayPal or a merchant account. Funds deposited in this way can be revoked if the credit card or account number is found to be fraudulent, and you have little or no recourse if you've already sent the product. If you're going to accept an international money order, it's better if it's issued by a reputable company like American Express. One of the safer ways to accept international payment is by wire transfer (this should be a separate account that you ONLY use to accept payments of this type). Remove the money from the account before you send the item.

Chapter 7

Spin Your Web: Selling Products From A Personal Website

Few things can make or break your online business faster than your website. Basically your website is the sexy salesman who could sell a ketchup Popsicle to a lady in white gloves. Formatting, content, and product descriptions are all important, but people are visual creatures, and ultimately the perception of the professionalism of your company and the over-all desirability of your product is going to rest on the aesthetics of your website. This is important whether you're selling homemade birdhouses or dropship-retailing kitchen appliances. Your products may bear the brands of reputable companies, but you still have to build an image of professionalism and security for your own business before anyone is going to supply a credit card number. We are going to talk a lot about what your website should look like, how it should function, and what it should contain, but first, how do you set up a website?

You may think the first step in setting up a website is designing your site, but this is like building a house before you've purchased a plot of land. The "build site" for your website will be provided by a hosting service or "hosting company". The hosting company provides space on a server they own or lease and they furnish Internet connectivity to your website. In addition, many hosting companies offer templates and tutorials to help you set up your website, and other services such as business email accounts, "shopping carts" for customers to make purchases off your site, and traffic-monitoring software. When choosing a hosting service there are a number of factors you want to consider.

1. **How proficient are you at web design?**

   If you are an absolute newbie who only just figured out how to check your email, then you are going to need a hosting service that caters to less web-savvy individuals. Your host may offer services such as tutorials, educational videos, tech support, and simple customizable website templates.

2. **What does the host charge for disk space and bandwidth?**

   Disk space is the amount of space allotted to you on the server to store your website. Bandwidth is the amount of space you have to transfer web pages from the server to the browsers of visitors to your site. The graphics and content you can put on your site are limited to the amount of space you are allotted. Keep in mind that while many hosts claim to offer "unlimited" disk space and bandwidth, they almost always have some restrictions like no audio or video downloads. Make sure to read their terms carefully or you risk having your website shut down or being charged more money. Signing up for "unlimited" space is fine if you needs won't be too high (you're not planning a second YouTube). If your needs will be greater than average, you will probably have to find a host who won't charge you an arm and a leg for extra disk space and bandwidth.

3. **How fast is your host's server and what is their uptime?**

Your website's speed and availability depends on that of your host. There's no easier way to lose sales and customers than to have your website crawl or refuse to load entirely. Be aware of the host's "uptime" – uptime is a measure of when a system is "up and running" as opposed to "down and not useable". Uptime is usually measured as a percentage, i.e. the system is up and running 99.99% of the time. If the uptime of a hosting service is only 99%, that means their system is down and inoperable for 14 minutes and 24 seconds per day. If their uptime is 99.99%, their server is only down for 9 seconds a day. (Uptime is usually calculated according to scheduled maintenance, so unexpected problems may add to downtime. Read online reviews to determine if a hosting company has more downtime than they admit to.)

4. **How many websites are you planning to operate?**

If you are planning to run more than one site in the future, you will probably want a hosting service who offers multiple domains and/ or IP addresses.

5. **What other add-ons are you looking for?**

Other services to look for from your hosting site are free software, unlimited email addresses, email forwarding, 24/7 tech support, and free photo galleries.

The following is a list of hosting companies who are highly rated by hosting review sites and consumer articles. If you want to research further, I would recommend getting onto the online forums to read posts from actual users. The prices listed are starting prices for basic hosting packages.

A. **Brain Host ($4.95**) – Environmentally friendly – powered by wind power. Brain Host has over 50 plus one click installs, such as Word Press. They offer free website builder tools, and also provide free traffic and SEO packages. Brain Host will also offer free transfer of domain, many companies do not do this.

B. **Fat Cow ($3.67)** – Highly rated for customer service and cheap pricing, as well as speed and reliability. Environmentally friendly – 100% powered by wind power. Fat Cow is the top-rated hosting site on multiple review sites with a satisfaction rating between 94-99%. Personally I find the cow-puns a little over the top ("Moo Crew Support, "Udderly fantastic prices", etc.), but it's their service that counts.

C. **Just Host ($3.95)** – One of the newer web-hosting services. Offers unlimited email addresses and domain names. Speed and reliability are highly rated. Just Host is rated second on multiple review sites with a satisfaction rating between 92-98%.

D. **IPower ($4.95)** – Offers tutorials to help newbies get started. Again, 100% wind-powered. They offer virtual servers for medium-sized companies not quite ready to make the jump to dedicated servers, but who require more resources than normal. They also provide a wide variety of scripts and features that make their sites more functional than many other hosts.

E. **Host Monster ($3.95)** – Considered one of the best in customer service with 24/7 support. They allow unlimited domain names on each account and have the disk space and high transfer allowances necessary for large websites. Their speed may not be quite as good as some other hosts. **5.Blue Host ($3.95)** – Also has a great customer service reputation (24/7 support). They've been in business since 1996 (that's like a hundred years in e-time). They allow you to host unlimited domains on each account.

F. **IX Web Hosting ($3.95)** – One of the only web hosting companies that owns and operates its own datacenter. They offer a one-hour support guarantee (a tech guy or gal will call you back within one hour of posting your request). They also guarantee that your hosting charges won't increase in future renewals. They allow large storage/transfer amounts, and each account has 8 dedicated IP addresses (which is pretty rare).

G. **Host Clear ($3.95)** – Also a newer company, but part of a bigger Internet media company called Just Developit. Their services include free website statistics, unlimited email, message forum software, and functionality scripts.

H. **Host Papa ($4.28)** – Also a green company. They offer 1 free domain and unlimited sub-domains.

I. **Go Daddy ($6.29)** – Their features include free email accounts, email forwards, forums, photo galleries, blogging, and pre-installed and add-on software applications. Their uptime may not be quite as good as some other hosting services.

J. **Yahoo ($4.99)** – Their hosting packages are geared toward beginners, and their support team is top-notch. The web builder is free and includes 100s of templates. If you are more experienced, you may find their packages limiting, but their servers are extremely fast. They only offer one domain per account.

Again, these are top-rated hosting companies, but they may not fit your specific needs. Be sure to research your hosting company carefully as they can have a huge impact on the function of your website. Also, I should mention that some pundits advocate using smaller, less well-known hosting services as they do not have as many sites hosted on their servers and thus their speeds can be faster. I don't disagree with this; if you know of a smaller hosting company you've heard good things about, by all means give them a try.

Once you've chosen a hosting company, you will need to purchase a domain name. The "domain" is the location of your website, the URL people are going to type in when they want to find your online business. You can pick whatever domain name you wish (as long as it hasn't already been taken by somebody else), but it's not a decision you should make lightly. Your domain name is one of your most powerful marketing tools. It's the first ambassador of your business, the first words that people associate with your company, so it needs to be strong and evocative. It's also the tool people use to find your website so it needs to be clear and easy to remember.

Tips for choosing your domain name:

1. If possible, you want your domain name to mimic the name of your online business as closely as possible. Thus, if your business is called "Bamboo Heaven", your domain name should probably be "www.bambooheaven.com".

2. You need a domain name with the most common suffix possible. There are a lot of different gTLDs you can end your domain name with, but the most widely known, and thus the preferred gTLD, is ".com". Unfortunately, a lot of the .com names are already claimed, from legitimate usage and also by people bogarting them for future resale. You really need to get a .com address even if you have to pay more for it or pick a different domain name than you were hoping for. If you go with .net or .org instead, you could lose an untold amount of business from people typing in the wrong suffix. A .com suffix is also important for your image since it is considered by far the most professional. If you do end up purchasing an old name, it can actually be beneficial to your SEO (Search Engine Optimization. If you want to be really thorough, you can purchase all the domain names for www.bambooheaven (.com, .ca, .net, etc,) and redirect so they all feed into your website.

3. Sometimes you can't use your business name as your domain name (maybe that domain name is already taken or your company's name would make for a long and confusing address i.e. "Aunty Ida's Notions 'N Things"). In that case, you might want to try a descriptor name like "www.sewing.com" or "www.embroidery.com". Most of these will probably already be taken, but you might get lucky. The benefit of a name like this is how short, easy to spell, and evocative it is. However, it doesn't promote your online business name. If you do decide to pick a domain name based off keywords, make sure it's not too long and that the keywords are placed in order (www.cheapcarparts.com, not www.carcheapparts.com). This is much easier to remember and prevents you looking dyslexic.

4. In general, you want to avoid domain names that are only acronyms. They're not descriptive, not memorable, and they have no keywords in them. It's better to have a somewhat long name "www.brandonmarshallconsulting.com" than the totally non-descript "www.bmc.com". Acronyms can also carry negative associations: if your online business was called "Katrina's Kandy and Kards", you definitely wouldn't want to go with an acronym.

5. Try not to use dashes or symbols in your domain name. You may be tempted to do something like "www.candy's-candy.com" simply because it's available, but that will be hard for people to remember. Also, if there's already a domain name so similar to yours that you have to add dashes, consider how many of your would-be visitors are going to end up at that other site. If your company name actually does have a dash or symbol in it, make sure you register both domain names, ("www.walmart.com" and "www.wal-mart.com") to cover all your bases.

6. If you're having a hard time coming up with a domain name, do a test run: tell your friends and family your online business name and ask them to guess what they would expect your domain name to be. Try giving someone your domain name over the phone and see how difficult it is for them to copy/spell. If people are misspelling your domain name in one or two common ways, consider registering those names and feeding them into your site as well.

7. Once you've narrowed down your prospective domain names, try typing permutations of them into the search bar and also the browser. If you're selling Christian Self-Help Books, and for some reason your prospective domain name is bizarrely similar to a bunch of porn sites, you should probably revise your plan; association is a strange and sticky substance. You also don't want your domain name to bring up a bunch of websites in close competition with your online business.

Most of the above comments can be applied as much to your business name as to your domain name (the admonition not to use acronyms, for instance.) I should also mention how much I hate businesses with crazy-spelled names like All-Starzz Shoos. I'm sure your mom told you it was cute, but it makes it difficult to find your company on a Google search, to refer it to friends, or even to remember it for future visits. Choosing a business name and a domain name can be a long and tedious process, but it's an important part of branding, marketing, and SEO, so don't just use the first thing that comes to mind.

Okay, now that you've got a place to build your website, let's talk about how you're going to do it. There are a few different ways you can get a website set up. Assuming you don't have the skills to build a website from the ground, you could hire professionals to do it. This would probably run you a couple thousand dollars, but would get you the best results. You might have to pay additional fees for updates in the future: the best way to keep these fees low is to have your web designer show you how to do some of the basic tasks like adding fresh content, adding/removing products, etc. If you want to get professional results for a much lower cost, consider hiring a student to do the work. They'll usually work for much cheaper, though you won't have the same recourse if you don't like something about the design as you would have using an established company.

You can find students by posting on Craigslist or on the notice board of your local tech/graphic design school.

A second option, which I've mentioned briefly before, is to design your own website using a template. The benefit of this tactic is template websites are quite easy to customize and cheap to procure (many web hosts provide them for free). Templates are easy to alter or update. The downside of using a template is you have to work really hard to make it look like it isn't a template. The last thing you want is for your website to be indistinguishable from another site your customer just visited; you think people don't notice when a company uses stock images and layouts, but they do. If you decide to go this route, make sure you put the time in to customize the template as much as possible. Also, consider purchasing high-quality images from an outside source if the ones in your image library are too generic.

When choosing a template, make sure it will fit all your needs before you invest time into customizing it. For example, one of my clients spent upwards of 200 hours designing his website before he realized how poorly the template fit his needs: it didn't have a search bar, drop-down menus, and worst of all, the shopping cart only allowed him to use one dropshipper. This effectively deep-sixed his whole effort as he relied heavily on three different dropshippers. Not all templates are created equal, so make sure yours has all the necessary features before you start work on it.

No matter which web-building option you choose, you are going to have to make some decisions about the layout and aesthetic of your website. I cannot overstate the importance of easy navigation and an attractive site. If the website is hard to use, visitors will give up. If it's unattractive or unprofessional looking, they won't purchase anything. The following are some web design tips to help you build a website that will knock people's socks off:

First: Make it Easy.

Pretend you're designing a website for a five-year old, because frankly, most five-year olds can shop online more comfortably than my 54 year-old mother. Not everybody is a computer whiz, and even people who are don't want to take the time to figure out your clever little button hidden inside your logo. If a shopper can't find the product or information they want, they're going to ditch your site and head to the next one. Contact information, shipping prices, products, articles, etc., should all be easily accessible, preferably from a simple toolbar on your homepage.

Above all, your website should have a search bar at the top of every page. That is my hands-down biggest site navigation peeve: when I visit a website, I usually know exactly what I'm looking for. I don't want to have to scan down a list of twenty different options and start clicking, hoping I'll end up in the right place. Finding a particular product is a twelve-step process on some people's websites, following a chain of never-ending links. It's much easier to simply type "China Dolls" in the search bar and be taken straight there. To check the facility of your website, get your most techno-illiterate friend to have a go at it.

Second: Simplicity is Beautiful.

There is always a temptation to cram as much stuff as possible into your website. I see this a lot on homepages because people want to make sure that if their visitor never gets past the first page, they'll still have seen everything the site has to offer. Products and prices, contact information, five photographs per square inch, blog excerpts, advertisements, everything but a mariachi band is piled on. Let me tell you something: the best way to make sure your visitor leaves immediately is to overload them on the homepage. The homepage should be a peaceful and attractive landing zone. It should clearly state the image and purpose of your business and offer a simple roadmap to the rest of the site.

Third: Be Creative, But Not Too Creative.

Of course you want your website to stand out from the pack. You want it to be eye-catching and unique, but there are some tried and true website standards you shouldn't buck. Shoppers are used to a certain layout: tool bar at the top of the page, or running horizontally down the side, contact info at the bottom of pages. search bar in the upper left-hand or right-hand corner. If you get too crazy with your layout, your website will seem bizarre or confusing.

Fourth: Color Speaks Louder than Text.

Aesthetics go far beyond a clean, simple website. From the moment your shopper gets on your site, they're judging your company and your products from visual cues as subtle as the color of your backdrop. You should carefully consider who your target audience is, and then determine what kind of colors, graphics, and fonts are most likely to appeal to them. Millions of dollars have been spent on this kind of consumer research, and you can profit by a quick survey of the kinds of colors your favorite brands use.

As a brief overview, bright, bold colors can excite your shopper and get them in a spending mood. But if your product is aromatherapy candles, you are probably better off with soothing pastels, which, incidentally, appeal to more to women. If you're dropshipping cribs and Baby Einstein products, use primary colors and cute graphics. But don't go over the top with themes: just because I'm buying an electric drill doesn't mean I need a harsh black-and-red scheme and Metallica music blaring in the background. As a rule, limit your palette to two or three colors that complement one another. Blue remains the most popular commercial color for a reason: it denotes professionalism, freedom, intelligence, and security. It is the most commonly listed "favorite color", but beware, it's also considered an appetite suppressant, and thus is not suitable for your caramel-apple boutique. Red indicates energy, strength, and passion, and often appeals to men. Green is associated with wealth and relaxation. Purple is considered sophisticated and luxurious. Black equals authority, elegance, and drama.

Two warnings about color: first, color will date you faster than a mullet and a pair of fuzzy dice. If you pick a trendy scheme, be prepared to update your website if your turquoise-brown combo goes out of style. Second, if you're selling to a lot of international clients, consider that color has different meanings in different countries. White is the color of death and sorrow in many Eastern countries, not the indication of purity and serenity it is in the good old US of A.

Fifth: Invest in a Logo.

Your logo is the distillation of your website. Your website proclaims who you are and what you can provide in clear visual terms, and your logo condenses that information into one simple, memorable point. There are many tutorial programs to teach you how to design a logo, like Alleba, or you can hire a graphic designer to create one for you (usually for around $200). A logo is particularly important if you plan to expand your business in the future. Consider the cache and force of a logo like Nike's: when Nike jumped into golf, the swoosh already meant something to golfers.

The key is to make your logo recognizable and attractive, but above all, readable. Don't use some crazy gothic script that even Robert Langdon couldn't decipher. And unless your name is Prince, you're probably not cool enough to have purely symbol-based logo just yet: stick to your company name or combine the name with a picture or symbol. One final thing to consider with logos: beside the visual appeal of simplicity, you may use your logo on letterhead and brochures in the future, and the simpler your logo is, the cheaper it will be to print.

One of the best ways to choose an aesthetic for your website is to check out comparable sites and see which ones appeal to you as a visitor. I recently did this exercise and it quickly became obvious to me that the most beautiful, appealing websites that gave the greatest impression of professionalism and elitism were the simple, bold, graphic sites. I was surveying wedding dress websites. This is an industry where aesthetics and professionalism are of premium importance since the bride-to-be wants to feel pampered and needs to trust that her dress will arrive on time, in one piece, and just as she expected it. Yet somehow I still managed to find an example of what not to do!

First, the website I absolutely loved: colettekomm.com. This site sells couture wedding dresses that a friend of a friend designs. Take a second to visit the site so you'll know what I'm talking about. The homepage is beautiful and utterly simple: a plain dark background, with a single black and white image of a hand cradling a lotus. Nothing else is needed, because this image evokes class, style, and natural loveliness, everything a wedding dress should provide without a wedding dress in sight. The logo appears with instructions to click and enter the site (I'm not crazy about the extra step, but I think it's appropriate for a couture site). A second image pops up of a girl in a wedding dress along with a simple toolbar of only four options: About, Collection, Press, and Contact. Very simple, very easy to choose which one you need to click on. Again, I like to see a search bar as well, but it's not a necessity for this site because it's so straightforward.

If you click on Collection, you see there are only 6 products. Because these are extremely expensive and exclusive products, only six are needed. Each product is displayed via three photographs, front, back, and close-up detail, with an impeccably written description. I won't copy the actual description verbatim, but this is the general idea: "The Floating Roses Gown: The bride emerges from a sea of delicate chiffon blooms, each one intricately crafted and hand-sewn, cascading from delicate buds at the neckline to open blossoms scattered along the train. An antique kimono silk lining provides a link with the past and a secret luxury for the bride of the future." Obviously this is a flowery and rather non-specific description, but selling wedding dresses is all about selling image and luxury, and in this respect it is the perfect product description.

No prices are listed, so you know the dresses are ridiculously expensive and if you even have to ask the price you probably can't afford them. This is the perfect touch of snobbery for Collette's target demographic. The lesson that applies to anyone is that price isn't always your main focus. In fact, when selling a niche product, it probably won't be. You need to figure out what your focus is and center your website design around it.

Now, the website I hated: http://www.shopforlover.com/. From the domain name you might think that this is a sex toy or lingerie website, but in fact it is a wedding dress site. This site isn't near as bad as some I've seen, but it's pretty crummy. Everything about it is cheap, crowded, and distracting. From the banner running along the top of the homepage to the kitschy hearts and unattractive factory photograph, nothing about this website makes me want to check out the products. The worst part is the blatant grammar and spelling mistakes. "Custom-Made and Tax-Exemption and Free Shipping For all dresses Abidingly!" the heading proudly proclaims. What the heck does that even mean? The sales pitch of this website is completely focused on discount prices, but I think you'd have to pay me to purchase a wedding dress off this site. It could be worse: the site has a search bar, tool bar, and livechat operator and there are no advertisements for other companies, but that's about all it has going for it.

Now that we've talked about the appearance and layout of your website, let's move on to some slightly more technical issues. A properly designed website is like a Venus Flytrap: sleek, efficient, intoxicating , and able to snag its victim in the blink of an eye. One of the main purposes of website design is to draw your visitor further into the site. If they never get past the home page, they'll never see the smokin' deal you're offering on organic diapers or the oh-so-witty-and-informative article you posted on jumping stilts. The following are some crucial website design tips to draw your visitor into the rest of the site:

Tip #1: Always format your website so it can be properly viewed on common browsers (Mozilla Firefox, Internet Explorer, Safari, Opera, etc.). There's no way visitors are going to download a new browser just to view your website.

Tip #2: Make sure your site can be viewed at any resolution: use stretch layouts that fit any screen resolution so all your visitors can see your website as it was meant to be seen.

Tip #3: Ensure that your website loads quickly: preferably in five seconds or less. Minimizing graphics, flash, and scripts, removing unwanted tags and unused scripts, and using SSI (Server Side Include) files wherever possible can help decrease load times.

Tip #4: Never put an "Under Construction" notice on any of your pages. You are going to be continually adding fresh content, products, links, etc. to your website. Posting "Under Construction" is like broadcasting that your site isn't ready yet, and implies there is nothing of value to be found there currently. Many sites remain "under construction" for months, years, or forever, so visitors are unlikely to check back in the future. Finally, search engines like Yahoo will reject your site if any pages have "Under Construction" posted on them.

Tip #5: Keep your text simple. Plainer fonts like Arial, Times New Roman, Calibri, and Verdana are easier to read and provide the simple, professional appearance you are trying to achieve. Further, a visitor has to have a font loaded in their system in order to see it properly, so if you use something really obscure people may not even be able to view it.

Tip #6: Don't assault visitors with background music. Like animation, background music makes your site load more slowly and is annoying and unnecessary to many (dare I say most) people. I often surf the internet while talking on Skype through my headset: when I click on a site that blasts music into my earphones drowning out my call, I am less than happy, and navigate away from that site immediately. It's even more annoying when the audio is some kind of sales pitch. Many of your visitors will find your site while at work, talking on the phone, surfing with their speakers turned up, etc. where unexpected sound will be very unwelcome. For an example of what I'm talking about, eat seven Krispy Kremes and then in a fit of remorse look up the Flirty Girl Fitness website where you will be subjected to cheesy pink noise, an extended intro, and the atrocity listed below:

Tip #7: Never use a "navigate away" box for a last minute pitch. Pop up boxes of any kind are Satan's leprechauns and should be outlawed. A box that pops up when I try to navigate away from a website shouting "Are you sure you want to leave this site? We have an amazing offer for you!" will never, ever prevent me moving on. In fact, I can't imagine anyone who would be swayed by that. It's just obnoxious, and sounds like a desperate huckster in a Moroccon bazaar.

So far we've talked about the aesthetic and function of your website. These are important, but in many cases the real efficacy of your website lies in its value to the customer. What are they getting when they visit your site? Great deals? Hard to find products? Tips and advice? Educational materials? A belly laugh? Community? You have to give something to get something: know what you're giving as well as what you're selling. Valuable content is important for another reason: it is essential for SEO (Search Engine Optimization), which we will talk more about in the next section.

What is considered valuable content and how can you add it to your website? Some of my favorite options include blogs, articles, product reviews, a Tip of the Day, forums/message boards, and newsletters. The key to valuable content is that it's informative, interesting, and non-promotional. A sales pitch for one of your products is not valuable content, though a non-biased product review might be.   Content should not be copied from other locations, and it should be updated regularly.

If you are absolutely awful at writing, you might want to consider hiring someone to write informative articles for you (many freelance writers are willing to work for as little as $10-30 per article).   You can also invite guest writers to pen articles for your site – this could be a blogger you admire, an industry professional, or a dedicated hobbyist.   (The benefit to the guest writer would be an inbound link to their website and/or some other form of promotion or credit).   The better your content is, the more effective it will be at attracting traffic, building customer relationships, and improving your SEO.

Chapter 11 will include a more in-depth analysis of SEO for your website, but there are a few basic steps you can take in the beginning.   The purpose of SEO is to improve your ranking on the SERPs (Search Engine Response Pages).   Your goal is to be in the top three websites that pop up when someone Googles "gourmet popcorn" or "beach towels".   It is extremely important to be at the top of the SERPs because of something called "The Golden Triangle".   Basically, what this means is that most people only read the first few listings, scan a few more, and then stop looking.   If you are marooned way out on page 5 of the SERPs, no one is going to find your website.

The first and most important way to help your SEO is to submit your website to all major search engines.   If you don't submit your website, it won't be indexed by Google, Yahoo, MSN, etc. – they won't even know it exists.   You can easily submit your site by going to the homepage of each search engine.   Remember, don't submit your site to the search engines until you've finished construction and you are ready to process orders.

The second simple thing you can do to improve your SEO is to have plenty of keywords on your website. Keywords are one of the main ways that fresh content helps your SEO: whenever you write an article or blog post for your website, include plenty of relevant keywords. Keywords are words that someone would search for when looking for a particular product or service. For instance, if I was looking for cake decorating supplies, I would search using the words "cake decorating", "cake design", "cake tools", "baking", "birthday cakes", etc. Thus, if you are selling cake decorating tools on your website, you want to make sure you have plenty of these keywords on your web pages. Just make sure you don't go overboard – stuffing your content full of keywords should never take precedence over clarity and quality. If you don't know how to choose keywords for your website, check out competing websites and see which keywords they're using in their titles, content, and metatags (the custom-written blurbs that show up under their link on the SERPs).

The final thing I want to talk about with website design is creating an image of security on your website. In order to make money on your site, you need people to hand over their credit card information, and there's no hope of that happening if your website doesn't offer an image of security. Customers begin to judge your website from the second the page loads. Within moments, they will have made a subconscious decision of whether your website is "safe" or "not safe". If it's the latter, you're not going to make a sale.

The first factor in creating an image of security is what we already talked about: a professional and attractive appearance. Nobody wants to purchase off a site that looks like it was designed in 20 minutes by a 14 year-old. An overload of flashing graphics, banners, and ads aren't just annoying, they look cheap and they sabotage your credibility. The more ads and extraneous links you have, the more you customer realizes that you aren't making your income off a quality product, but rather by advertising and affiliate links. Most online shoppers have surfed hundreds of websites. They are aware of the standards for retail sites, even if only peripherally. If you fail to meet standards, it will be painfully obvious to all but the most novice shoppers. Above all, your content needs to be direct, competent, and completely free of spelling and grammar mistakes. Nothing is a faster give-away of amateurism than sloppy content.

Third-party security icons are a quick and easy way to build an image of safety. Companies like TRUSTe will review your site: if your payment methods, etc., meet security standards, they will allow you to post their icon on your site. Keep in mind, your security has to be legitimate in order to qualify – you can't just pay your fee and get the icon. These security sites claim that retail sales increase between 7-12% once their icon is posted, which could be well-worth the monthly fee to retain their services.

Finally, protect your site. Once you've gone to the trouble to build a unique and well designed website, the last thing you want is some shmuck ripping it off, destroying your credibility with their crummy clone site. Make sure your images and content cannot be copied by a simple right-click of the mouse.

This is far as I'm going to go into web design at the moment. However, there is another aspect to selling products off a personal website: getting people to your site in the first place. This is known as bringing in traffic. You can attract traffic by improving your SEO so that any time people Google a relevant keyword, your site pops up at the top of the list. However, SEO can take time because it relies in part on the age of your business and website. If you don't want to wait a year or two to start making money, you can build traffic quickly by advertising.   Advertising online is much more affordable than traditional methods like TV commercials and bill-boards.   Chapter 9 will focus exclusively on marketing your online business, including bringing traffic into your website through Pay-Per-Click advertising, banner ads, and social media marketing.

Chapter 8

Think Outside The EBay Box: Selling Products From Other Venues

EBay is the most popular place to sell products online, but it definitely has its downside: fees, hefty competition, and a mass of listings that can make it hard to get your products noticed. For certain kinds of products or simply to get free of the pack, you might consider using a different online venue.

The following is a short overview of some of the other places you can sell products online:

1. **Bonanzle**

Bonanzle is supposed to be sort of the anti-eBay. It's a venue to sell more unusual, off-beat items. There is no charge to list items, and selling fees are a lot cheaper than eBay. Bonanzle tries hard to promote buyer-seller communication, so there is a lot of instant-messaging and "pervasive chat" on their site, which amounts to more real-time negotiation. They also have a "pre-schedule pickup time" program for people who want to sell items in their own city and avoid shipping costs – this could be beneficial to you if you're interested in selling a large, bulky product that can't be shipped conveniently. Finally, their customer service is much better rated than the largely hated eBay customer service team. Overall, Bonanzle has been rated the best eBay alternative by Ecommerce Guide and Small Business Computing.

The downside to using Bonanzle, like any alternate venue, is they don't command quite the same traffic as eBay, so you may not get the same volume of sales (though you can easily get lost on eBay and not get any sales there either). I do know of at least one person who opened a t-shirt store both on eBay and on Bonanzle, and received multiple sales from the former, but none from the latter. (This could have been influenced by the fact that most search engines don't rate duplicate content, and many Bonanzle sales come from Google listings).

2. Craigslist

Each major city has its own Craigslist site, and items are posted in a fixed price format, no auctions. Craigslist is better known as a place to find a job or a free couch, but you can also make money selling products here. My sister-in-law made a quick hundred bucks the other day re-selling a German Shepherd puppy. She posted the listing early in the morning, and it was gone by 11:00. No list fees, no percentage of her profits retained by the website. (Now this wasn't exactly a voluntary sale: her husband bought the puppy fully intending to keep it, until he woke up with a face resembling an inner tube, and realized he's allergic to dogs. But the point remains: they made money buying a product on Tuesday and reselling it on Wednesday.)

Some of the major caveats to Craigslist are as follows: First, a lot of scams a perpetrated on Craigslist as on any site, and you have to be careful: buyers do not have to open a Craigslist account or be verified in any way to respond to your posts. You should especially be cautious about people purporting to be from Spain, Africa, etc., who "just need your bank account number to send you a wire transfer". Second, you might have to stick to selling to people in your own city because most Chicago Craigslist buyers assume they are buying a product from someone else in Chicago and may well want to come over and see it before forking out their cash. Finally, Craigslist is not set up to be your own personal eBay store, so if you post fifty different items for sale, you'll probably get blocked as a spammer.

3. Amazon

Amazon has removed its auction option, but you can still sell items in the Stores section. Amazon has no listing fees, and is probably just as popular as eBay is. (This means there is also a lot of competition, just like on eBay.) Amazon is known more as a place to purchase new products vs. used ones, but those are likely the kinds of products your average dropship-retailer would be selling, so that's not necessarily a negative. Amazon also has a lot of options for order fulfillment: for instance, they will act as a dropshipper, storing, packing, and shipping your products if you send them a bulk shipment. However, they will also slap their name and logo all over the box, since self-promotion is somewhere between catnip and crack for Amazon.

4. ECrater

ECater is patently designed to be similar to eBay. The main benefit of eCrater is their dedication to remaining entirely free – no listing fees, and no final value fees. They make their money by charging for premium product positions. Whether this means your listing will be practically invisible if you don't pay, I don't know. Like most of the alternatives to eBay, it's a little soon to find definitive feedback on the message boards, and successes and failures have a lot to do with individual sellers' decisions.

5. Online Auction

Onlineauction.com is one of the auction sites that allows you to pay a flat fee to list as many products as you want. In this case, it's $8 a month. Onlineauction.com is one of the similar-to-eBay sites that users switched to during a recent spate of eBay boycotts. While I have received positive feedback from some people who made the switch, others have not yet sold anything from the new venue.

There are a huge number of alternate venues for sell products online, and it's difficult to say which one will be the best for you. You may have to try a couple of sites before determining which suits your style and your products. Experimenting is easy since most have much lower fees than eBay, or are entirely free.   I would certainly recommend checking out other venues as it may be easier to get a foot in the door as a new retailer. The downside to these alternate sites is that probably only one or two will ever become as successful as eBay and Amazon, and the others may well fade away to nothing. But there's no law that you have to choose only one venue: you could hedge your bets and sell your products on a dozen different sites if you have the time and the multi-tasking ability.

Below are a number of other eBay alternatives I've heard good things about:

Adflyer.co.uk – a British alternative

Altec Trader – No fees except for specially promoted listings and the option of a free store

Audiogon – Place to buy and sell used hardware, flat fee of $8 per month

Deal Tent – Listing fees and commissions apply, but cheaper than eBay

Etsy – Place to buy and sell any handmade products

iOffer – An auction site with no end times and a lot more haggling

My Store – No fees except for advanced seller features. Simpler to use than eBay.

Neoloch – Calls itself "The Friendliest Auction Site"

Overstock Auctions – Extremely similar to eBay, one of the best-looking sites

Trocadero – A storefront for antique and fine art sales. No listing fees, flat fee of around $30-45 per month

Wagglepop – Also a flat monthly fee of $9.95

Chapter 9

Billboards and Balloon Boys: Marketing Your Online Business

Everybody knows that marketing is an important part of business, but what exactly is marketing? Marketing is a process by which you obtain and retain customers. You create value for the customer and build a strong relationship that allows you in return to get value from the customer. There are three basic steps in marketing: drawing the customer in, securing and satisfying them, and obtaining return visits from the customer. Obviously, the focus at all times is the customer. How can you attract them? How can you satisfy them? And how can you keep them coming back? Apparently marketing is a lot like dating, but even if you were never a success with the opposite sex, you can succeed in business because online business allows you complete freedom to recreate yourself. You can tailor your business in a manner that will captivate your target demographic.

The first step in marketing is to create a marketing plan. A marketing plan is an imperative part of your business plan, which you should develop one in the early stages of setting up your business. This plan is something you will refer to and continue to tweak as long as you are operating your business. Writing this plan out in full allows you to articulate the aims and tactics of your company and helps keep you focused. Your business plan/marketing plan will also be useful if you need to attract business partners, apply for loans, or convince suppliers to work with you.

Your marketing plan has five basic sections:

1. Define your target market.

Who will buy your product? If you answer "everyone" to this question, you're probably wrong. Even cheeseburgers don't appeal to everybody, so don't be afraid to specialize. Figure out who you want to sell to, and then zoom in on them like a shark chasing a surfer in a seal-blubber suit. Your target market influences all your marketing decisions, because marketing to the blue-hair set is quite different than selling to single parents or status-conscious teenagers. In fact, a recent study by Sarah-Jayne Blakemore of University College London indicates that teenagers use an entirely different segment of their brain to make decisions than adults do (the mentalising network, vs. the prefrontal cortex) - so apparently you can't even appeal to a uniform set of neurons with your marketing scheme. Defining your target market allows you to focus your efforts on a distinct person, not some amorphous customer whose needs and preferences you can't imagine.

2. Determine the specific benefits of your products or services.

This step should be done in conjunction with step one. Determining what benefits your product or services offer helps you to decide who would appreciate those benefits, and thus who you should market them to. Conversely, knowing your target market helps you to know which benefits to highlight and what uses a product or service could be put to. So work on these two steps together.

3. **Plan how you will position your products/services.**

In marketing, "positioning" means creating an image or identity in the minds of your target market. Positioning can focus on your company image, your brand, or your specific product. For example, if you are selling baby shower gift baskets, are you trying to position your product as fun and exciting, chic and elite, or an absolute necessity for the new mother?

4. **Formulate your company's Unique Selling Proposition (USP).**

The USP is a marketing concept proposed by Rosser Reeves of Ted Bates & Company to explain a pattern of success among advertising campaigns in the early 1940s. His theory states that the campaigns made unique propositions to the customer that convinced them to switch brands. Basically, the USP differentiates a company or product from other similar companies or products. Ted Bates & Company carried out a market research study that identified two successful elements of the USP: penetration of the market, and usage pull. Usage pull can also be considered the "unique selling point". For example, when Head and Shoulders sells their shampoo, their unique selling point is their product gets rid of dandruff. They don't focus on the softness or shine their product can provide as most other hair-care companies do. If you are dropship-retailing lingerie, your unique selling point could be, "Make his jaw drop", or, if you want to focus on the company image instead of the product, maybe something like, "If you're not happy, we're not happy" (focusing on your image of customer satisfaction). A slogan can be the best way to encapsulate your USP.

5. **Determine your marketing methods.**

Now that you know WHAT you're going to market to WHO, and HOW you're going to do it, WHERE are you going to market? What venue will you use to promote your website and your products? Blogs and reviews? Message boards? Online ads? Direct marketing (a system where you bypass intervening media and attempt to send messages directly to customers, i.e. by e-mail campaigns, newsletters, phone calls, etc.)? When formulating your marketing methods, you need to determine which techniques work best on your target market and with your specific product. Social networking sites can be a great advertising venue for hip trendster products, but a waste of money if you're trying to sell orthopedic shoes to grannies.

Spend time on your marketing plan, really think it out. When you're finished, don't just shove it in a drawer somewhere: review your plan at least once a quarter and see how well you are adhering to your goals. Don't be afraid to alter those goals if experience reveals a flaw in your thinking; maybe you'll notice that an unexpected number of customers on your scented lotion website are men. When new information arises, alter your marketing strategy accordingly.

The first phase of marketing is attracting customers. This will be our primary focus in this chapter since step two, supplying value, is something we've already discussed in terms of having quality products and valuable content on your website, and the third step, garnering repeat business, will be examined in the next chapter when we talk about customer service and marketing to current customers. I really can't overestimate how important attracting customers and bringing traffic to your website is. Unlike a brick-and-mortar establishment where customers walk in off the street, nearly everyone who finds your website has to be directed there in some way, whether from your search engine ranking, pay-per-click advertising, a banner ad, or word of mouth. Active promotion is the only way you will get business.

One of the major ways you'll attract customers is through SEO. If you can get your website to the top of the search engine pages, you will automatically bring in a boatload of traffic. However, SEO is extremely time-consuming and can take a long time to get going. Even if you do everything perfectly, some elements of SEO rely on the longevity of your website and are impossible to rush. In the meantime, you can pay for exposure on the SERPs (Search Engine Response Pages) through Pay-Per-Click Advertising.

What is Pay-Per-Click (PPC) Advertising?

Pay-Per-Click advertising is an online advertising method where business owners pay every time their ad is clicked (usually on a search engine results page). The amount you pay for each click depends on how much you bid (you decide ahead of time how much you will pay for each visitor). The search engine page your ad appears on depends on the keywords you selected. You can agree to pay a set amount, say $400, and once you've received enough visitors to exhaust that payment your ad automatically disappears. This means you won't be surprised by thousands of visitors and thousands of dollars in charges.

How does PPC work?

Unlike many forms of advertising where you pay simply to post your ad, with PPC advertising you only pay for traffic that actually clicks on the link to come to your website. This doesn't mean your visitor will necessarily buy anything, but at least you've got them in the door.

What does PPC cost?

PPC can cost between a few cents and a few dollars per visitor; usually you bid for the best positions on the SERPs.

Where will my ad show up?

The link to your website will appear on the top and / or sides of the SERP as a sponsored link.

How can I get the most efficient PPC advertising?

First, make sure you bid for the top 10, or preferably top 3-5 spots on the SERP. Remember the Golden Triangle: if you're not at the top of the SERPs, it takes a very dedicated searcher to find you. To make sure you are at the top, you have to outbid the other people in your category. This won't necessarily cost a lot of money; you only have to outbid them by a penny per click.

Second, put yourself in the right categories by using the right keywords. Don't use keywords that are too general: you may end up with a lot of traffic, but your traffic won't have a good conversion rate (your visitors won't actually buy many products). Use specific keywords that accurately describe your website and products so the people who arrive are genuinely interested in your site. They will be much more likely to buy your products, so the traffic you paid for will be more profitable. To illustrate, if you have a cake decorating supplies website, don't use general keywords like "kitchenware" or "bakeware". Use "cake decorating" or even "fondant", "molds", "cake stands", "imprinters", etc. You can use keyword suggestion tools to help you select the right keywords.

Third, make sure you only pay for PPC advertising through major search engines (Google, Yahoo, etc.), and opt out of any non-search traffic. You want to make sure that the people visiting your site are actively looking for what you're selling.

When should you use PPC Advertising?

- Pay-Per-Click is important at the launch of your website when you need to get traffic flowing quickly.
- Pay-Per-Click is great for limited-time or seasonal promotions.
- Pay-Per-Click is important when testing ads and promotions because you can measure results easily.
- Pay-Per-Click advertising can give you a boost during slow periods.

When should you practice SEO?

- SEO is something you need to be doing consistently all the time.

SEO is a long-term process and you won't necessarily see results immediately. It can be less expensive than Pay-Per-Click because many aspects of it are free (though time-consuming), so SEO is something that you can plug away at when your advertising budget is depleted. Initially you may not see as many results from SEO as you will from Pay-Per-Click advertising, but over time as your search engine ranking rises, it can be a consistent and low-cost way to bring in traffic.

Other than PPC and SEO, there are many inexpensive or free ways to advertise your online business and bring traffic to your website:

1.Free Classifieds

There are a ton of online classified ads where you can advertise your business and products/services for free. Craigslist is one of the biggest and most widespread.

2.Newspaper Coverage

Call your local newspaper and ask if they would like to do a business or human interest piece on your online business. If you are running some kind of charitable event or interesting promotion, they will be more likely to find you newsworthy.

3.Car Decals and T-Shirts

Buy a huge decal for your car with the name and address of your website. Pass out fliers at the mall. Print a t-shirt with your business name and website and wear it everywhere until it starts to smell and your spouse won't come near you. Attend tradeshows and networking events and pass out your business card like candy – in fact, pass it out WITH candy so people are happy to get it. You may sell your products to people across the globe, but you can start the buzz right at home in Boise Idaho.

4. Advertising Swaps

Find a non-competing complimentary business and ask if they would like to trade banner ads. For instance, if you are running a teddy bear website, trade banners with a china-doll website. If you are operating a kitchenware business, find someone who sells home decor.

5. Use Your Networks

Starbucks once ran a campaign where they offered a free iced cappuccino to employees and their family members. They had to shut the offer down when the emailed coupons spread like wildfire all over the country. Try sending a coupon or special offer to friends and family, and ask them to pass it along to everyone they know. You'd be amazed how wide your network can spread, and how much traffic this could bring to your business if the offer is desirable or interesting enough.

6. Submit articles and guest blogs to directories and other websites.

You can include a link to your website, and if the articles are informative and helpful, people will be prompted to check out your site. You'll already have established a sense of trust and professionalism that will make visitors feel comfortable buying from you.

7. Post in forums.

Again, you can include links to your site. If your posts are intelligent and/or informative, people will check out your site. Don't be spammy about this though; individuals who frequent message boards and blogs are very internet-savvy, and they won't be fooled by naked sales pitches or stupid comments.

8. **Use free advertising sites.**

These sites generally work on a kind of exchange/credit system. They make money trying to get you to upgrade to paid advertising, but the free level works pretty well.

Some free advertising sites include:

http://www.trafficswarm.com
http://www.BannersgoMLM.com
http://www.MyViralAds.com
http://www.dont-touch-my-ads.com
http://www.web-dawg.com

Another way to advertise your online business cheaply is using social media marketing. Social media marketing is the act of using social influencers, media platforms, and online communities to market a business or product. Not every venue of social media marketing is going to work for your particular online business: to be effective, you need to consider your target demographic and tailor your social media marketing so it hits the right people. Social media marketing is fairly new, yet has already been complicated by companies that sign up for Twitter and Facebook and bombard everybody with spam. The key to social media marketing is making a genuine connection with people and then engaging in reciprocity – when somebody retweets your article or refers somebody to your fanclub, thank them and return the favor.

To illustrate how social media marketing can help you, I'm going to use a success story, namely that of Cathy Curtis of Curtis Financial Planning. Cathy attributes a great deal of her business' success to social media marketing, and you can learn a lot by reading her guest blog on Kristen Luke's site:

http://kristenluke.wordpress.com/2009/03/18/a-social-media-marketing-success-story/.

Cathy Curtis' Story:

Cathy started her own financial planning business, determining that her marketing position would be to shuck stodgy conventionalism for a more fun, approachable, creative image. Her target demographic was women. Cathy researched various financial planning websites to discover what appealed to her, as a woman in her target demographic. Since she liked bold, solid-color, graphic websites, that's the format she used for her site. Her unique selling proposition included a "10 Simple Truths About Money" program prominently featured on her website.

Once her site was in place, she joined a number of women's networking groups including eWomen Network, the National Association of Women Business Owners, and Ladies Who Launch. After attending various seminars through these organizations, Cathy was inspired to open a Facebook Business page called "Women and Money". She posted educational videos on her page to generate interest. She also joined LinkedIn and Twitter. On LinkedIn, you can search for professionals in specific industries, which is how Cathy was contacted for two write-ups in the Wall Street Journal. Other opportunities such as speaking engagements, magazine articles, and client referrals arose from her social media marketing efforts. Cathy also used social sites to stay in touch with colleagues and potential clients she met in person.

Cathy is a perfect example of how you should use social media marketing: you start with a great website, and then promote your website by joining social sites. You attract interest on these sites by participating in dialogues and posting helpful educational materials. When you market through other venues, you use your social media presence to solidify relationships.

The following is an overview of some of the most popular social networks, and ways that you can use them to promote your online business:

A. YouTube:

YouTube is a site where anyone can post short videos for free. Try posting instructional videos for your product. If you have a jewelry-making website, then post videos of how to make a custom charm bracelet or a pair of dream-catcher earrings. Provide a link back to your site where people can purchase the materials you used in your project (this would be a good opportunity to make a "kit" to sell multiple items at once).

B. Twitter:

One of the primary uses of Twitter is to show a company's "personality" through "tweets" (short posts). Twitter can also be used to post links to educational articles, or ask questions and post answers. Using TweetDeck, you can search keywords relevant to your business and find people searching for information related to your products.

C. Ning:

On Ning you can build a social network around anything you like. It's free, unless you want to restrict advertising, and then you have to pay a monthly fee. If you're selling yoga clothing or survival equipment, consider starting a social network for yoga lovers or people who believe the end of the world is nigh.

D. Facebook:

On Facebook you can build a personal profile with status updates, photos, message boards, email, and more. Anyone with a Facebook profile can add a Page to extend their content, which you could use for a Business Page for your dropshipping/wholesaling website. Potential customers can post on your message board, and you can add educational videos and product reviews, set notifications for upcoming industry events, and so on and so forth. Besides your Business Page, consider starting a community group like "Duckhunters" or "Gourmet Chefs of Chicago" (even though you can easily market country-wide or even internationally on the web, there's nothing wrong with focusing some of your marketing efforts on your specific geographic location – those are the customers you know best, after all). This will allow you to get in touch with people who share your interests and need your products.

E. LinkedIn:

This is a website for professionals to post profiles (like Facebook, only business-centered). LinkedIn is an excellent resource for connecting and staying connected to business contacts, and also functions as a kind of Yellow Pages. Jobs and business opportunities are also posted there. The main benefit of LinkedIn is that people can easily find your business and services, but you may use it yourself to search for suppliers, web designers, etc.

F. Blogs:

Other people's blogs are a great way to get your products reviewed or to build inbound links to your website. Bloggers are generally communicative people who welcome comments and requests for guest blog posts, interviews, etc. Due to the principle of reciprocity, if you make an intelligent and insightful comment, they may allow some kind of link in the post. But nobody likes spam or pushy requests, so don't spam post or behave rudely if they're not interested in working with you. If you manage to annoy a blogger in your attempt to catch their interest, they may ridicule you in their blog instead of promoting you. Check out the following article by Susan Getgood for submission etiquette and a few common pitfalls of communicating with the mercurial blogger: http://getgood.typepad.com/getgood_strategic_marketi/2008/07/batter-up-bad-p.html.

Social Media Marketing is a legitimate and sometimes even inspired way of marketing your online business. It's usually much cheaper than other forms of promotion (often free, other than the time expenditure), and it seems poised to keep growing and growing. You'd be wise to get yourself plugged into the network. However, a word of caution: everything you say and do on these sites is open to the public and recorded indefinitely. Make sure you always, always behave in a professional manner, even if you are approached by someone informally. Take care not to post any confidential information, and consider what incriminating evidence you are posting on social sites not directly linked to your business, like that photo of you dressed up as Britney Spears on your personal Facebook page.

The last thing I'm going to talk about is newsletters and eBooks. Most traffic that comes to your website you will have paid for in one way or another, through PPC, banner ads, etc, so the most profitable thing for you is to not lose any of these leads. Even if a visitor doesn't buy anything when they come to your site, you can lure them back by getting their information the first time around. One of the best ways to do this is to have a newsletter visitors can subscribe to, or an eBook that they can download for free. If you get their email address in return for the newsletter or eBook, you can send them a coupon or promotional offer to entice them to return. The important thing here is to attract, not annoy, your customer. A simple coupon for 10% off or free shipping, or a "Thank you for visiting, come back and view our Back To School specials", is sufficient. You do NOT want to pelt them with spam emails and above all, never ever sell their information to somebody else. This is a promise you should make at the time of gathering the email addresses so people aren't afraid to hand them over.

I'm sure everybody is familiar with the Balloon Boy hoax from last year. The Balloon Boy is an example of marketing gone horribly wrong. The Heenes had some kind of science show they wanted to promote, so they constructed a giant weather balloon as a taster. That's not a bad idea: where there scheme crashed and burned is when they pretended their son was trapped inside, wasted public money on a pointless rescue operation, and buried themselves under a mountain of lies. You can't trick people into giving you their business. If you try to bring them to your website through false keywords and meta tags or misleading promotions, it's only a matter of time until they figure out the scam, at which point you'll not only lose their goodwill, but will incur their active loathing.

I really can't stress this enough: if you want to run a successful business, you need to have quality products and quality content. You need to give people something of real value. Then they'll be happy to spend their money, come back and spend more money, and refer you to all their friends. Marketing isn't about fooling people into visiting – it's about getting people in the door so you can blow them away with the real value of your online business.

Chapter 10

Keep 'Em Coming Back For More: Building Your Repeat Business Percentage

Once you've attracted customers and dazzled them with your fabulous business operations, you want to make sure that you're continually building your repeat business. One of the best ways to do this is to have an excellent customer service/complaint resolution program.

While I was in school I worked as a waitress at a high-end steakhouse in a historic mansion in Toronto. The wait staff's motto was the aforementioned "Every customer leaves happy". No matter what we had to do, every customer walked out the door with a smile on their face. This meant that sometimes we provided free drinks or dessert when people waited a long time for a table. Sometimes our manager made the rounds apologizing if the kitchen was running slow or an order was mixed up. One time we provided a whole tableful of guests with $50 gift cards after a waitress spilled a bottle of wine on them. The restaurant occasionally lost money on a particular table, but I can guarantee you nobody ever went home and told twenty friends about their awful experience.

A lost customer can cost you a lot more than the potential sales that one person would have constituted. They might tell five friends how awful your website was, they might give you a negative rating on eBay, they might even blast you on a message board. One disgruntled customer can have a larger detrimental impact on your business than you expect. For example, look at the movie Avatar: when it was released in December, it didn't break any kind of record on its opening weekend - it had a solid but not mind-blowing debut. However, its second weekend broke the record for raking in cash – which I would credit entirely to word of mouth. Everybody who loved Avatar told ten friends they absolutely had to see it in theaters, and they did. Within a few weeks Avatar became the fifth movie to break the billion-dollar mark, and the fastest one to get there.

Though you're courting positive word of mouth, keep in mind that you can't please everybody. Despite your best efforts you will inevitably tick someone off (for every ten sweet little Charlotte Churches there's a Mariah Carey just waiting to explode if you don't pick every last purple Skittle out of her candy bowl). However, most customer issues can be resolved through good communication.

5 Tips for Complaint Resolution:

1. Be Available.

When someone is already annoyed by your product or service, the best way to make them furious is to neglect to have a "contact us" or "customer service" button on your website. The optimal situation is to have a phone number where they can call and speak to someone directly, but if that isn't tenable for your business, an email address will suffice. If you go this route, be sure to state clearly that "questions and comments will be answered within one business day" (that means you actually have to do it). If you decide to go the livechat route, please for the love of heaven get an operator who can type quickly. When I contacted Bloomex to complain that my aunt's birthday orchids were never delivered, I could have driven up to Canada and dropped the flowers off myself in the time it took the operator to type her response (see – and now I'm publically criticizing the company).

2. **Don't Judge The Validity Of The Complaint.**

Maybe the complaint is a solid one: the laptop you sold them arrived with a smashed screen. Maybe it's entirely spurious: they don't like the color of the box it came in. It doesn't matter. Whatever the complaint is, it obviously bugged your customer, and might cause them to delete your address off their toolbar and slander you on every message board they can find. Don't try to tell them it doesn't matter; figure out how to fix it. Which brings us to tip #3:

3. **Have A Policy In Place.**

You don't want to be inventing something on the spot while an irate customer is screaming in your ear. Also, you don't want to be bullied into promising something unreasonable. Have a plan in place for common contingencies so you can calmly and kindly inform your customer that the company's policy in that instance is to...

4. **Be The First To Suggest A Solution.**

Don't wait for the customer to tell you that they want a full refund. Instead, offer a replacement product, a discount on their next order, or whatever policy you've decided on. Sometimes, an apology is all that's necessary (in case of poor service, for instance). Offering a solution will help diffuse the situation by assuring the customer that you are taking their complaint seriously and will work to resolve it. Asking what they would like you to do opens the door for them to demand maximum recompense.

5.   Be Polite, But Not A Punching Bag.

To put it bluntly, some people are jerks. It doesn't matter what you do for them, they're still going to leave with a bad taste in their mouth. This is just my opinion, but you don't need the business of that tiny minority and you probably couldn't keep it even if you wanted to. So I would never sit and listen to a string of profanities or threats. You can calmly inform the customer that they are welcome to call back once they've cooled down, and hang up the phone.

Customer service is the backbone of any strong business. In online business, resolving complaints is often the only direct contact you have with the customer, since you're not physically there when they find your website and order the product. Usually the point where you have direct contact with a customer is the point where they call to complain, so use that opportunity to wow them and boost your repeat business percentage.

Besides word of mouth advertising, a positive customer experience is integral to receiving repeat business. Repeat business is so important for the health and profitability of your online business. Every customer that you receive will cost you a dollar amount in PPC advertising, SEO efforts, and other marketing ploys. Thus you want high conversion rates (you want visitors to actually buy something), and you want customers to return again and again, because it doesn't cost you any money to get them in the door a second and third time.

For an example of repeat business success, look at Scott Griggs of the eBay Store Trainz.

Scott's Story:

Scott opened his eBay store in 2005. While he had had some success with a brick-and-mortar business, high overhead costs were cutting into his profit. Selling on eBay allowed him to maximize his time and profit margin. As his eBay business grew, Scott implemented an approximately 70% auction style, 30% inventory listing format. He sold his expensive and unique model train items auction-style and used the inventory format for add-on purchases, accessories, and slower-selling items. A mix of formats helped garner exposure for his eBay store as well as improve average sale prices. High percentages of auction-style listings brought in new customers, while immediate sale formats appealed to his repeat customers. Scott also encouraged repeat business (which accounted for at least 35% of his sales), by sending friendly, personal email newsletters to all his customers. This helped build business relationships, and also functioned as an advertising tool. He also provided repeat-customer discounts. These policies, combined with his impressive shipping practices which included shipping notifications and tracking numbers for each sale and his commitment to resolving all customer complaints to the *customer's* satisfaction, helped him maintain an astonishing 99.5% positive feedback rating. His sales in 2006 topped $2 million.

There are two kinds of consumers in this world: people with brand loyalty and people without. Most of your repeat business will come from the former. These brand-loyal customers are extremely important – marketing guru Philip Kotler asserts that brand loyal "heavy users" account for up to 80% of sales. (This is due to the

Pareto 80-20 Rule which states that 20 percent of users accounting for 80 percent of usage — and of suppliers' profit). Gaining loyal customers is usually a result of three steps: making a connection, providing value, and establishing trust. A connection isn't made simply because a customer comes on your website and purchases a product. Rather, they connect and become brand-loyal when something about the experience goes above and beyond their expectations and emotionally touches them.

The most recent company to which I made a connection was an online t-shirt retailer called Threadless. Threadless did a number of things absolutely perfect in order to snare me: first, I saw their ad on Facebook. The enticing promise of "All Shirts on Sale $10!" prompted me to click the link, something I've never done before on Facebook. Once on the website, I was captivated by their humorous and unusual t-shirt designs, all of which were indeed on sale for $10 as promised. The design of the website was attractive and easy to navigate, and a number of dropdown menus were cleverly labeled to direct me to areas of the website I wouldn't have searched out on my own, like the "fantasy" and "nerdy" sections. Once I made my order, the products arrived promptly and were of high quality.

Now, all these elements of Threadless' online business were very well orchestrated. But how did the site really make a connection with me? Something small and simple – the t-shirts were modeled by other customers. When you buy a shirt off threadless.com, you can take a picture of yourself wearing it and they'll post it on the site. People have gotten extremely creative with this, like a werewolf t-shirt modeled by a girl being chased down the street by a vampire. This simple marketing technique makes it obvious that Threadless likes to interact with their customers – it's not a faceless corporation, but rather a company run by real people with a sense of humor who actually like their customers.

The thing you can really learn from Threadless is that they did EVERYTHING right – if the website had been annoying to navigate, if the order was screwed up, if the shirts were lousy quality, I wouldn't have showed the site to a bunch of other people, or ever gone back again. You can't *just* carry good products or *just* offer a friendly newsletter - you need to hit on all cylinders to secure brand loyalty from your customers.

The last thing I'm going to talk about is trust. As I said before, an image of security is extremely important on your website. Another element of trust is not abusing the information your customers give you. If you gather emails or referrals, never pelt the people with spam or sell their information. A thank you email when a customer orders from you, or one or two coupons or special offers a month is quite sufficient. It drives me nuts how sends me emails practically every day. One mention of "People who liked Bill Bryson's *A Walk In the Woods* also liked…" was nice. Getting one every other day makes me want to burn the books they're recommending. If you do run a newsletter or email coupon campaign, make sure there is a button for receivers to opt out of your promotional emails .

Chapter 11

Pruning the Roses and Mulching the Tulips: Growing Your Online Business

Let's assume your online business is now up and running: you have a couple of fantastic suppliers, some great products, your website is operational, and you've been practicing basic SEO, purchasing Pay-Per-Click advertising, and stocking your website with quality content. You may or may not also be selling on eBay, but you are definitely making sales and brining in money, if only on a small scale. The next step is to grow your online business. With the basics are in place, you can focus on more advanced business and marketing initiatives.

The first thing we're going to talk about is somewhat more advanced SEO techniques. Basic SEO involves regularly adding fresh content, using keywords, and submitting your website to all the major search engines. These are really the bare minimum elements of SEO: there are dozens of other things you can and should be doing.

1. **Submitting to Directories.**

A "web directory" or "link directory" is a directory of websites, some commercial and others not. The directory links to sites and categorizes the links so the searcher can click on something like "Jewelry" and find websites related to jewelry – sites that sell engagement rings, sites with jewelry-making tools, museum sites with exhibits of crown jewels, etc . The websites are not organized by keywords, only by category and subcategory. A website is usually limited to inclusion in only a few categories.

Most directories require the website owner to submit their site for inclusion. A directory editor reviews the submission and determines whether the website will be included in the directory (they are primarily trying to weed out spam websites that are little more than an excuse for ads). There are general directories and niche directories, and both are useful to submit to. Some offer free submission and others require reciprocal links or paid submission (usually a one-time fee, sometimes a recurring fee). Additional fees can get your site more prominently featured in your category.

The benefit of submitting your dropshipping website to directories is that it will bring in traffic, help attract inbound links, and possibly aid in SEO (Search Engine Optimization). Not all directories help with SEO, but the best and biggest directories are given some weight by Google and other search engines.

When submitting to directories, make sure you follow the instructions very carefully, or they probably won't accept your site. Directories, especially the free ones, receive thousands of submissions and editors lower their workload by automatically deleting submissions that don't conform to their requirements. Each directory is different, so don't assume you can read the rules at one site and then copy and paste for all the others.

The best directories to submit to are those that are highly ranked in the major search engines (niche directories need not be quite as highly rated as general directories). Also, check to ensure that your prospective directory isn't banned by Google. Directories get banned for a variety of naughty practices: while the directory's banned status probably won't affect your site, why take the chance? Also, one of the benefits of directories is their inbound link to your site, and the value of that link is determined by the prestige of the directory, so a banned directory won't help you in this respect. Even if a directory is not highly ranked on the SERPs (Search Engine Response Pages), you might consider submitting anyway because its ranking could change, and if your website is prominently featured in the directory due to its smaller size, that could be helpful. But don't bother to pay for directories that aren't highly ranked.

Finally, submissions may take months to be accepted, especially with free directories, so don't expect to see results tomorrow.

The following are some of the more prestigious and popular directories on the Internet:

A. **DMOZ (dmoz.org)** – DMOZ is one best directories and one of the only top dogs that is still free to submit to. Your acceptance to DMOZ will help with SEO, traffic, and backlinks. It provides legitimacy to your business and helps you attract advertisers. The only downside to DMOZ is that it could easily take 6 months or more to get listed depending on your category and how meticulously you format your submission.

B. **Web World Index (webworldindex.com)** – This is a paid directory with a cost of about $25/year. As with most paid directories, your approval time will be much faster. Be sure to check this site's requirements as it has some unusual ones including the need for your website to have a current mailing address posted.

C. **Yahoo (yahoo.com)** – "Standard" submission is free, but expedited acceptance costs $299 annually. This fee is required for all commercial sites. Yahoo is one of the biggest directories on the net (a rival to DMOZ) and the backlink you receive from Yahoo can help your SEO.

D. **Pegasus Directory (pegasusdirectory.com)** – Pegasus is a free directory. Their approval time is moderate and they are quite highly ranked with Google. Many users have reported receiving backlinks as a result of their Pegasus listing.

E. **Jayde (jayde.com)** – Another free directory, with a surprisingly fast approval time. It's a little crowded though, so try to apply to a less saturated category.

F. **Best of the Web (botw.org)** – BOTW charges a $49.95 annual fee or a $149.95 one-time fee. A listing in this directory with help your SEO. You can pay additional fee to be a "category sponsor" which will get you listed at the top of your category.

G. **Link Centre (lincentre.com)** – This directory costs $49.95 annually (euros, not dollars). They practice automatic approval, so your submission will be accepted, but as with many automatic directories, you'll have a lot of competition.

H. **Canlinks (canlinks.net)** – This directory is for Canadians specifically. Americans can use it too if they're trying to market to Canadians.

This is not a comprehensive list of directories, but simply a list of those I've heard good things about. There are many other directories worth the 5-15 minutes it will take to submit your website. I haven't really addressed niche directories here because there are so many and their worth depends largely on your exact product, but don't forget about them - niche products require niche marketing, including directory submission.

Now, how do you get your website accepted to the best directories?

- Make sure you follow all the submission guidelines to the letter. They are usually different for each directory, so read the guidelines thoroughly and don't make any assumptions.

- Make sure your submission is well-written and without grammar or spelling mistakes. Mistakes will cause delays in your acceptance and prejudice editors against you.

- Compose a concise title and description for your submission that are not stuffed with keywords and are not a blatant sales pitch. Pretend you're making your own directory with informative (and reasonably objective) blurbs for each website –that is the tone you need to use.

- Submit to the right categories and only the right categories – If you submit to too many or inappropriate categories, the editor may disregard you application.

- Ensure that your homepage is professional, has useful/informative/valuable content, and is not overloaded with ads. Many websites submitted to directories are spam sites, filled with useless or rip-off content that is only an excuse to post a mass of ads. If your website resembles these it will probably be axed after a cursory glance.

Directory submission may or may not make a huge difference in bringing traffic to your website. It largely depends on which directories you get accepted to, and whether you product is one that people generally search directories to find.

2. Building Inbound Links

Another important element of growing your business is building inbound links or "backlinks". I touched on this in the previous section when I said that inbound links from directories could help your SEO.

What are inbound links? There are a number of different links on a website: internal links (from one page of your site to another), outbound links (from your website to someone else's), and inbound links (from other people's sites to yours). Inbound links are the most important for two reasons:

First, inbound links bring traffic to your website. If I'm reading a blog on how to lose five pounds in five days, and your website is listed as a place to buy guarana supplements, I can click on that link, come to your website, and buy my guarana.

Second, inbound links are part of the algorithm that determines how your website is ranked by search engines. Depending on the engine, inbound links are weighted more or less heavily. Google's search engine is sophisticated enough to judge the quality of the links as well as the quantity. The ranking of the website linked to yours and the relevance of your respective materials are both considered.

How do you build inbound links? Including unique, interesting, relevant, helpful, funny, and generally desirable material on your site will naturally prompt people to link to your website. If you post information worth knowing and disseminating, then people will link to your site so they can share it.

You can also solicit inbound links by asking another website to review your products/services, or by guest blogging on another website. When you guest blog or leave a comment on someone else's blog, it is often appropriate to include an inbound link. For example, if I was reading a blog where the benefits of seaweed wraps were being debated and I happened to have an article on exactly that topic on my site, I could leave a comment saying, "I think that seaweed wraps are extremely beneficial for reducing cellulite – here's a link to an article that talks about how I lost five pounds using seaweed wraps." Most bloggers will allow these kind of links, but if you leave a stupid spammy comment, it will probably be rejected.

You can also use reciprocal agreements to build inbound links – for instance, trade links with a fellow small-business owner. You need to be extremely careful when trading inbound links. Plenty of people will try to get you to join "link farms" or networks where a hundred people are all linked to each other: this will actually have a negative impact on your SEO, and could even get you banned from some search engines. An inbound link from a crummy website doesn't help you anyways – you want links from sites that are equally or better ranked than yours.

When you do receive useful inbound links, find out where they're coming from and see if you can get more of the same type. For example, if you run an organic coffee website and you notice you've gotten a few inbound links from gourmet foodies, then nurture that relationship. Set up a message board, a series of articles, or a gourmet products section that will appeal to your new demographic.

Also, show your gratitude. When you receive a great inbound link, like a positive review of one of your products, make sure to send a thank you email to the source. This may help prevent the link being broken a few days later, and also helps cultivate the business relationships that are as important in the e-commerce world as they are in regular retail.

Finally, don't forget to redirect. If you change the address of any of your pages, be sure to redirect all links so you don't lose the benefit of existing backlinks.

Learning how to cultivate inbound links can be challenging, but the more popular your website gets, the easier it is, like rolling a snowball down a hill. So chip away at this important aspect of SEO, and if you do your job right, soon people will be linking to your website without you doing anything at all.

3. Use Long-Tail and Short-Tail Keywords

When covering basic SEO we talked about the importance of keywords. Keywords can be further divided into "long-tail" and "short-tail" keywords. A short-tail keyword would be something like "cowboy hats" while a long-tail keyword would cater to a more specific niche like "rhinestone cowboy hats". Use long-tail as well as short-tail keywords to capitalize on both widespread and specific customer groups.

Also, when writing your website content be aware that keyword density is important, as is the proximity of keywords. This means the more keywords of a particular type in each paragraph, and the closer those words, the higher search engines will rank you for that keyword.   Many search engines count synonyms as well as the keywords themselves, so "footwear" is helpful when your keyword is "shoes", but synonyms are not as important as the primary keywords. There is a limit to how many keywords you can insert, however – keyword density over 10% is a Black Hat SEO technique known as keyword stuffing and could get you banned by search engines, so it's pointless even if your only goal is to generate traffic. Your readers also won't enjoy it - ultimately your content is written for your customers more than the search engines, so make sure SEO doesn't overwhelm the quality and relevance of your writing.

Finally, some people will recommend that you misspell some of your keywords to try and catch people who misspell them in searches. In my opinion you should never do this, not even in meta-tags. It makes you look unprofessional and it's an affront to the beautiful and functional English language.

If you're having trouble coming up with keywords, you can try using the following tools:

A. **Google   Adwords** (https://adwords.google.com/select/KeywordToolExternal): Type in one or two descriptive words for your products and Adwords will list keywords, their search volume for the last month, and their average search volume. Besides finding potential keywords, you can use Adwords to check the keywords currently found on your site. If you copy your dropshipping website URL into the Website Content box and click "Get Keyword Ideas", Adwords will tell you all the keywords found at your URL.

B. **Overture** (http://sem.smallbusiness.yahoo.com/searchenginemarketing /): Overture is a good tool to use, though it will only show you information on searches done in Overture and only for up to a month's time past. Still, what is highly-searched in one engine is very close to what is highly-searched in the others. Overture's Search Term Suggestion Tool will show you variations of the original keyword, which can be helpful for choosing other keywords and also for composing content. For instance, if you type in "cake baking" as your first keyword, and you see that the top search result is "cake baking tips", than you know you should probably have a blurb on your site devoted to exactly that topic to bring in traffic.

C. **Wordtracker**

(http://freekeywords.wordtracker.com/gtrends/): Use their free trial to search for keywords. Wordtracker, like Overture, will show you words or phrases related to the primary keywords you are searching.

D. **Trellian** (http://www.keyworddiscovery.com/search.htm): If you enter your example word, Trellian will generate the top 100 relevant keywords.

4. Give Meta-Tags Their Due Attention

A lot of people don't bother much with meta-tags because they generally don't affect your SEO, but I think they're important anyway. Meta-tags are the blurbs that appear under your website title on the search engine response pages. That's the blurb that an actual human being looks at when deciding whether they should click on the link and visit your site or not. A meta-tag should be a brief and accurate description of the webpage in question. It's important to make your meta-tags as effective as possible because getting yourself on the top of the search page isn't enough – you have to get people to actually click the link.

5. Monitor Your SEO

Check your page ranking regularly using tools like the Search Status plugin for Firefox. Google checks over 200 parameters when ranking your site, so there are a lot more things to consider than the elements of SEO I've touched on. If your site isn't getting the ranking you want, consider paying for some help. Have a professional review your site and tell you what you can still work on. But don't just throw money at the problem: learn yourself. SEO isn't going away. It's an important skill you need to develop and continually practice. It's not something you can master with money anyway; no company or individual knows SEO perfectly, so nobody can do it all for you. Also, every website needs a personalized strategy, and a lot of SEO companies use a formula which may have a mediocre level of success for your site.

6. Avoid Black Hat SEO

I mentioned that keyword stuffing is Black Hat SEO. There are a number of SEO initiatives that fall under the category of "Black Hat" and should be avoided. Determining what exactly is "Black Hat" is sometimes like asking which fouls should be called when the Lakers play the Cavaliers - there may some bias when it's your website in question. Though definitions vary, the idea is that "Black Hat" techniques are those which are fraudulent or deceiving, while "White Hat" SEO techniques are honest, industry-accepted, and promote a better experience for the website visitor.

Websites that use fraudulent Black Hat techniques generally have no real, relevant product to offer. The focus is to earn money, without providing value in return. You should never try to trick people into coming to your website. If you want to attract traffic, you'll have to do it through legitimate information (blogs and articles), services, and products.

It's also important to know whether your SEO initiatives are considered Black Hat or White Hat, because if search engines catch you using the former, they will blacklist you. The last thing you want is for Google to stop listing your website.

How do you know what is acceptable SEO?

First: Does your SEO jibe with the experience of the visitor? It's important that you don't misrepresent your website. Your meta tags and keywords should accurately represent the products and services your website has to offer. For instance, one "Black Hat" SEO technique is to sneak a bunch of keywords onto your website in places where they are invisible to the visitor. You could hide a whole string of white keywords in your white background; crawlers pick up the keywords, but visitors do not benefit from actual relevant content.

Second: Are you breaking guidelines? Not all guidelines are clearly spelled out, and sometimes search engines change what they deem acceptable. But basically, Black Hat SEO deliberately exploits weaknesses in search engine algorithms and breaks search engine guidelines in order to get better results. Make sure you are complying with any and all guidelines of the engines you submit your site to. You can win the game playing by the rules; you don't have to cheat to get your website top-ranked. It may take a little more work to maximize your SEO through solid, traditional techniques like building inbound links, but it's better than wasting your time trying to trick the engines.

Ultimately, the terms "White Hat" and "Black Hat" are somewhat ambiguous. My opinion is that if you are honestly representing yourself and your services, and what you provide is truly of value to the customer, than you don't have anything to worry about.

7. Engage in Deep Submission.

Often you can get the best SEO results by focusing on web pages individually. In a sense, each page of your site is like its own website. This is particularly true of sites that cover a number of topics or themes. Say you operated a notions website: you might have separate pages for knitting, embroidery, cross-stitch, rug-hooking, etc. Each of these pages would be like its own website. Each page would bring in its own visitors who searched for keywords like "embroidery thread" or "latch hooking".

How can you take advantage of the unique nature of each of your web page? First and most importantly, you want to submit individual web pages to directories and search engines. You can't submit your pages all at once or they'll be tagged as spam, but you can certainly submit one web page URL per week to each of your targeted directories or search engines. This is known as deep submission, and is extremely important because search engines generally do not look at every page of your site when ranking you – some don't make it past the homepage. Your homepage doesn't cover all the relevant topics and keywords contained in your website, so you need to make sure your other pages are considered. While it's not necessary to submit pages that won't help your ranking, you definitely want to submit all pages with valuable content and plenty of keywords. This will help your SEO and will bring traffic to specific, targeted parts of your website.

Since visitors will be coming to various web pages, you need to make sure every page is an efficient landing zone. If people are landing on, say, your blog or newsletter or Tip of the Day section, you want to make sure they still see the rest of your website. Make it easy for them to navigate to the homepage and any product pages. Have a search bar at the top of each page. Ensure that contact information is visible at all times. You can even have an option for them to sign up for your newsletter or email offers at the bottom of each page.

Remember meta-tags in deep submission. You need to write specific meta-tags for each page of your website following the guidelines listed above.

You can also create extra pages with an eye towards deep submission. If your website is currently quite homogenous, consider making separate pages that you can individually optimize. For instance, if you have a hiking gear website, consider making separate pages for local hiking in your area, hiking in exotic locales, and maybe a survival tips section. This kind of diversity allows you website to appeal to a wider range of people: it casts a net to capture traffic you might never see otherwise.

Now that we've talked about some ways to engage in more in-depth SEO, I want to talk about other ways to grow your online business. First, let's talk about monitoring your website statistics. How will you know if your SEO efforts are successful? How will you know which advertising campaigns are really working for you? Obviously a rise in sales is a good indication, but how can you tell which of your initiatives is responsible for that rise, and which are the weak areas of your website? Monitoring your website statistics can provide the answers to these questions.

Many web hosts provide free website statistics. Depending on your website host, those stats may be sufficient, or you may want to pay for a more in-depth look. Companies like WebStat and Deep Log Analyzer will provide comprehensive website statistics for about $9.95 per month. If you decide to go with an outside company to provide your stats, make sure your results will be simple and clear so you're not also forced to pay for an analyst to decode them.

What can website statistics tell you?

A. You can find out exactly where your visitors are coming from. If the majority of your traffic comes from SERPs (Search Engine Response Pages), then you know your SEO is solid. If you are paying for directory listings that aren't bringing in any traffic, then you know you should axe that investment.

B. You can monitor which browsers your visitors are using. If most of your visitors have a different resolution setting than your site, you know you need to make changes so they can view your website properly.

C. You can see how long visitors stay on your site. If you're receiving a lot of traffic, but people aren't sticking around for more than a minute, you know your site isn't providing them with the valuable content they expected, or perhaps your site is too difficult to navigate.

D. You can analyze your conversion percentages. Your conversion percentage is the percentage of your visitors who actually buy something. If your traffic is strong but your sales are weak, somehow you're not closing the deal. Checking your exit pages can demystify this phenomenon: if your product pages are the exit point, then either your products are shoddy or your prices too high. If people bail on your check-out page, then your shopping cart check-out is too complicated, or your shipping prices are turning people off.

E. You can monitor traffic spikes. If your traffic and / or sales increase after a particular marketing campaign, then you know you should repeat that initiative. This helps you focus your efforts so you don't waste time and money on SEO, ads, or marketing that isn't bringing dividends.

If you're not checking your website statistics regularly, you're doing your business a grave disservice. A lot of online sales are blind in the sense that you don't see or speak to your customers or receive much feedback. Checking your stats is a way of keeping yourself present in your online store so you know what's going on.

Now I want to take a more in-depth look at a few of the ways you can add valuable content to your website. First, adding a blog. This is something I've mentioned a number of times in this book, because I think it is one of the best ways to continually add content to your site and build a connection with your customers. The idea of writing your own blog may send you curling into a little ball with flash-backs of tenth-grade English class swirling around you like the Ghosts of Christmas Past, but this is something you'll have to get over, because content-writing is a necessary evil until your online business is lucrative enough that you can pay some other schmoe to crank out copy at two cents a word. Beyond necessity, your blog is the go-to guy of your website, the Handy Manny who can do a dozen different tasks at once, and do them well. Who knows? You may actually enjoy tapping the keys when the topic is something you're passionate about. The benefits to your website will probably endear you to blogging even if nothing else does.

What should your blog cover? Whatever you want, really. As long as your content relates to your products and includes keywords, the sky is the limit. If you've got a kitchenware website, fill your blog with favorite recipes, funny anecdotes about the soufflé that ruined your last dinner party, reviews of the new Kitchenaid mixer, tips on how to make the perfect crepe, and so on and so forth. As you begin to accrue comments, coming up with topics will be that much easier - at least half the blog articles I write come from a question or comment someone made on the WholesaleRelations.com website. I also get a lot of ideas from news and events in the industry. You definitely want your blog to be current, so I would recommend reading other people's blogs and scanning sites like Forbe's e-business news page. You'll want to do this anyway so you can find appropriate places to make your own comments and leave links back to your site.

The important thing to remember with blog articles and any other content is that your writing has to be more than a bunch of words strung together on an in-demand topic: it really needs to help people. Nothing annoys me more than clicking on a blog with a title like "How to find DVD dropshippers" and the whole article is a lot of nonsense like "try to find DVDs that are in demand". Duh – that's obvious, and has nothing to do with finding dropshippers. Your articles and tips need to impart information of value, or they're just a lot of words strung together. I would refuse to buy anything or click on an affiliate link on a website like that out of principle.

A blog can also be a secondary source of income. If you get enough traffic, you can sell a small amount of advertising space on your blog. You never want to go overboard with the ads because it makes your website look trashy, but two or three well-placed and relevant ads can bring in significant income. You can use a tool like Google AdSense to automatically select relevant ads for your website. Related to this is the option of affiliate marketing, which will be the subject of the next chapter. Affiliate marketing involves placing a link to a related but non-competing site on your website. When people click on that link and purchase a product, a portion of the sale goes to you. A blog can be a great asset to an affiliate income, because you can write directly about the products being sold by the affiliate partner. For example, one well-known blogger makes the majority of his income by writing a blog about the best gifts to give hard-to-shop-for individuals, and then posting affiliate links to the products he recommends.

You can also make extra income by joining a paid blogging network. As a member of these networks, you can bid to write reviews for products. You publish the review, send the link to the company, and are paid between $50-200 per post (Note – the blogging networks take a percentage of your earnings). There are multiple networks you can join, including PayPerPost, Review Me, and Sponsored Reviews. This is another way of increasing your income while simultaneously improving your SEO and adding value to your dropshipping website.

Not everybody is going to be able to make subsidiary income from their blog because not everybody is a competent writer, and to join the blogging elite like Perez Hilton (who charges $75,000 a day to advertise on his site), and whoever it is that writes the hilarious "Stuff White People Like" blog, you would have to be a pretty talented wordsmith, not to mention skilled at self-promotion. But even a very basic blog can be a platform for content and help boost customer relations, so I would highly recommend including a blog in your website design.

A second thing you could consider adding to your website is a forum or message board. A forum or message board can help bring in traffic and build relationships with your customers. Adding a forum to your website is a great way to build a community of return visitors. If you are using social media marketing, a forum is particularly appropriate.

What is a forum?

A forum is a web page where visitors can interact with each other. They can leave messages and comment on other people's messages.

What are the benefits of a forum?

Beside the aforementioned traffic and sense of community, it helps imbue your website with solidity and professionalism. Further, a forum can be extremely educational. You always want to provide valuable content on your website, and with a forum, other posters will help provide this content by answering each other's questions (this also helps your SEO). Also, a forum helps you keep in touch with your customer base. If you see people talking about a particular product or service, you can be sure to get it on your site. Thus you can stay on top of the trends by reading your own or other people's forums. Finally, a forum is a good place to put a little subtle advertising in the form of banner ads, links, etc. to bring in extra income.

How do you install a forum on your dropshipping website?

Many website hosting packages actually come with an option to add a forum to your site. If yours doesn't, you can get a script that will set up and run a forum, and install it on your web hosting server. Some are free; the more complex ones cost money. Installing it can be a little tricky, so unless you are quite computer savvy, you will probably have to pay somebody to do it. The easiest thing is to use a host who provides it.

What are the possible negatives of a forum?

Besides the potential difficulty of setting up your forum, it can be challenging to build interest. When visitors check out a forum with few posts, they aren't motivated to add anything themselves or visit again. Try and get friends and family to post on your forum to get the ball rolling. It's important to have a lot of in-depth industry-related posts because that is also how most people find forums – by Googling a question and finding the answer on the forum. Finally, managing a forum can be time-consuming. You want to restrict the posts as little as possible because people are unlikely to return if their post gets bounced. Unless you have a family or children-friendly website, you probably shouldn't delete posts for a little profanity or inappropriateness – save your veto power for the really offensive stuff. However, you'll get a lot of spam posts that are thinly-veiled advertising from individuals and spam bots, and you'll want to remove that junk.

There are two more elements of growing your online business I want to talk about. The first is a marketing technique: crafting an image of success for your online business. At every step of your marketing process, from designing your website to sending out customer newsletters, you need to make your online business look like a multi-million dollar company. Why is this important? Because an image of success and professionalism makes people feel secure. They feel secure in choosing your company, and they feel secure in handing over their credit card number to purchase your products. Whether your online business is well-established with multiple employees, or whether it's just you working out of your mom's basement in your underwear, your company can look like it's run by Steve Jobs.

1. **Website:**

    The first and most important factor in making your online business look posh is your website. I've already talked about attractive web design, so all I'm going to say here is that you need to avoid an excess of banner ads, affiliate links, and other extraneous advertising on your site. Customers should get the impression that it's your quality products that make you money, not ads.

2. **Web Address:**

    Again, you already know the goals for your web address. Your URL should contain your company name and not much else. If it's a bowling website, your address could be delancybowling.com or delancybowlingballs.com. A long and convoluted URL stuffed with keywords is hard to remember and looks cheap – so no delancybowlingshoesshirtsandballsforcheapprices.com. Real e-business giants are branded, so they can make URLs as simple as amazon.com. Keep your URL as strong and simple as possible, and make sure you get a .com suffix.

3. **Contact Information:**

Your contact information should always be prominently displayed, and the more contact options you have, the better. You should have a phone number where customers can contact you directly, if at all possible. Even better is purchasing a vanity number. A vanity number is a phone number that spells your company name or service. For instance, your bowling company's number could be 1-800-DELANCY or 1-800-BOWLING. Like a memorable web address, a vanity number helps bring in business because customers can easily find you or refer their friends to you. Also, it looks fancy and legit on your website. Happily, vanity numbers can be purchased for about $50. You also need to record a professional-sounding voicemail. State your business' hours of operation and that the customer can expect a call back within one business day. If you answer the phone personally, never, never have loud noises or screaming kids in the background.

4. Professional Packaging and Shipping:

Make sure you purchase professional packing materials and print custom labels. This doesn't have to be expensive; for instance, if you're selling off eBay, there are multiple apps to print packing and shipping labels. These programs will also help you keep track of your packages. Make sure you always ship products in a timely manner, and if there is any delay, email or call your customer to inform them.

5. Formal Communication:

Whether communicating over the phone, via email, or in person, maintain your professionalism. Make sure all your emails are concise, polite, and free of spelling or grammar mistakes. When communicating over the phone, never, never use profanity. Nothing brands you as unprofessional more quickly than dropping an F-bomb. It's also extremely offensive to some people, and not just prudes. Profanity includes religious references; many people are offended by the use of OMG though they might not say anything.

6. **Business Address:**

Depending on your product (one that requires a stringent image of elitism), if you are operating a home-based business from Armpit, Nebraska, you may want to purchase a more prestigious address. Mail-forwarding services can make it appear that your business address is on Wall Street if you so desire. This is known as a "virtual office" and will cost your business about $200-400/year.

7. **Business Cards:**

Even though your business is online, don't forget to utilize traditional marketing techniques like sprinkling the city with your business cards. Make sure your business card adheres to the same bold, simple graphics and font as your website, and ensure that your web address is prominently featured. Also, I would recommend clearly stating the product or service your company provides. I know a lot of businesses like to use the curiosity mode of marketing, posting huge billboards with just their name and address, but that doesn't work with people like me who don't remember it later and don't have time to

Google every random company they come across. I believe a direct, simple statement like "Quality Bowling Supplies" on your business card will do your company the greatest service.

Finally, the last element to growing your online business that I am going to focus on is preventing fraud. Fraud can take a huge bite out of your profits and can lose you customers. No website or eBay account will ever be entirely protected from fraud: for every new security measure put in place, there's some kid fueled by Bagel Bites and internet porn trying to hack his way through it. But there are a few simple measures you can take to boost your defenses:

Tip #1: Post an anti-fraud statement on your website and assure would-be scam artists that you will prosecute them to the fullest extent of the law if they attempt to place a fraudulent order.

Tip #2: Use email verification before shipping orders. Send the customer an email with a link that they must click on before the order is processed. This helps ensure that the information they provided you with is accurate. But make sure that you inform the customer that the link will be sent BEFORE they place their order, otherwise you might lose legitimate orders of people who are spam-paranoid, or receive irate calls from customers who didn't check their email until three days later.

(Note: Some fraud experts will suggest that you do not accept orders from people with free email accounts, since the free accounts do not confirm that the personal information provided is correct. But a lot of consumers use yahoo, hotmail, gmail, etc., and don't have a paid account, so you could easily slash your sales in half by rejecting their purchases.)

Tip #3: Have a system in place to confirm that the shipping address matches the billing information for the credit card (you can access the bank database for this). Apple is an absolute stickler on having this kind of information match up, and they frequently review their orders and flag any with suspicious elements, contacting the customers directly before shipping. Again, you run the chance of annoying customers who are simply using, say, a business credit card, but in this case the annoyance is more than balanced by the security. You can explain to any irritated customers that this measure is for their own protection to assure that someone is not using their stolen credit card. You can subscribe to a service who will monitor orders for you.

Tip #4: Don't be fooled by phishing. "Phishing" emails are those that purport to be from your bank, credit card, PayPal, eBay account, or other trusted source. They "phish" for information by saying something like, "we just need to confirm some information from your account... if you could please send us your Social Security #/birthdate/checking account #, etc, etc." Never respond to this kind of email. Banks and other legitimate sources do not ask for information this way. You can also protect yourself by using different email accounts for PayPal, eBay, and customer service email, so if you receive a PayPal email to your customer service account, you know something is amok. As a seller on eBay, you may receive phishing emails disguised as queries about a product you've posted. Sometimes the information they are seeking is something as simple as your direct email account. If you always access your eBay email through your eBay account, you can communicate without giving anything away.

Tip #5: Don't be fooled by pharming. "Pharming" is a little more tricky. This is a practice by which you are directly to a dummy website that looks exactly like a trusted website. Its sole purpose is to get you to plug in personal information. It's very easy to imitate a website as, by nature, almost all elements of a website are downloadable. You can avoid pharming websites by never clicking on links that pop up in suspicious places, and always typing in the web address directly. Many web experts consider the pharming threat highly overrated, but it's something to be aware of.

Tip #6: Check the security of your website. Use a company like GamaSec to test how secure your website is. Testing companies will scan your website for common vulnerabilities, and provide you with an analysis of each aspect of your site. The scanner launches a series of simulated attacks and notes how your site responds, so the test is quite accurate. The analysis will include recommendations of how to improve the security of your dropshipping website.

It's not my wish to contribute to the fear-mongering that often reigns on the internet, but by educating yourself about common methods of attack and common defenses, you can lower your chances of being blindsided by fraud on your dropshipping website or eBay account.

Efforts to grow your online business will continue as long as you're operating your company. At some point you may want to start a second or third or fifth website, or open an eBay store or two. Only you know when you're ready to expand your efforts. Just make sure you don't over-extend yourself – you always want to have a substantial cash reservoir and enough physical help that you can continue to give each customer premium service. The cash reservoir is more important than I can stress – there are plenty of businesses that go under not because they're not making money, but because they're cash-poor. At certain times there may be a lot of money going out and something may interrupt the money coming in, say a website crash or a block on your PayPal account; you need to have enough money set aside to cover dry periods and handle contingencies.

Chapter 12

The Mythical Cash Cow: Affiliate Websites

I'm starting this chapter with some trepidation because in point of fact I don't like affiliate websites. When I Google "vintage Adidas sneakers" and, due to a misleading meta-tag, I end up on an affiliate site that's nothing more than a bunch of links to other places that sell Adidas sneakers, I invariably hit the back button to return to the Google SERP. Even if one of the links is a store I actually want to visit, I'd rather find it through Google than click the link and send a portion of the sale to somebody who tricked me into visiting their site.

In my opinion, affiliate sites that are nothing more than a collection of links are parasitic. They're lazy; no effort is made to provide something of value to the visitor, so I don't want to provide the owner with any profit.

Now, this doesn't mean that I think you should never build an affiliate site, or you should never include affiliate links on your blog or retail website. Rather, I think if you want to make money off affiliate marketing, you need to do it right. If you don't do it right, you're probably not going to find affiliate marketing a profitable venture anyway.

Affiliate marketing is one of the most misunderstood money-making schemes on the internet. Hard-core advocates are always promising that you can post a few links on your website, then sit back and watch the commissions roll in. As with most online business ventures, the potential for profit is there, but it's not that easy.

What is affiliate marketing?

Affiliate marketing is a system where you apply to the affiliate programs of various online businesses, then set up a link between your site and theirs. When visitors click the link on your site to access the affiliate sponsor site and purchase a product, the sale is recorded and you receive a commission, between .5 and 12% of the sale, usually.

How do you apply for affiliate programs?

It's quite easy, actually. Many websites have a link at the bottom of the page to apply for their affiliate program, or you can apply for programs en masse using databases like Popshops, CJ.com, Linkshare, or the Google affiliate network. The Wholesale Relations Research Team can find affiliate programs for you, or if you have a company you absolutely love, you can call them directly to determine whether they have an affiliate program you might qualify for. Once you've decided which programs you want to apply for, send your application, and the company will accept or reject your application, usually within a few days. (Acceptance can be immediate or contingent on an examination of your website).

A lot of people are drawn to affiliate marketing precisely because it's so easy to get into. You could apply for hundreds of affiliate programs in a day, post the links on your site, and wait for the cash to show up in your bank account. But you might be waiting a long time. As anyone who has rashly built an affiliate site can tell you, you could wait months and end up making about $6. Why? What goes wrong?

The problem is, while you can post the links on your website, you only make money if people click on those links and purchase products. So you have to do two things in order to be successful: you have to bring traffic into your website, and you have to convince that traffic to click on your links and make purchases.

We've already talked about bringing traffic to your website through SEO and so forth, so let's focus on how you can promote affiliate links. Again, it all comes down to valuable content. Valuable content is important for any site, even one that carries legitimate products with an appeal of their own. With affiliate marketing, content is everything. Not only do you have to provide something worthwhile to your customer, but your content needs to specifically reference your affiliate links more than regular product-related content does. For instance, if you were operating a designer diaper-bag website, you could post articles on almost any baby-related topic: diaper rash remedies, teething horror stories, the best organic baby food, etc. However, if you operate an affiliate site with links to designer diaper bags, you would want at least some of your articles to more specifically address the products: "Diaper Bag Of The Year: You Could Actually Come To Love Dirty Diapers", for example.

This kind of direct reference to the product is a "call to action" or endorsement of the link. You need to be at least a little subtle: putting some text that says "Hey click this link!" or "This product is awesome!" isn't going to work. However, if you write an informative and extensive review of the product, then post your affiliate link at the bottom, your chances of getting clicks are pretty good. You can also change or rotate your affiliate links to align with your articles. For instance, you could write a blog on "The Best Mother's Day Presents" and temporarily post four or five affiliate links for the specific products you reference in the article.

A second way to promote affiliate links is to sell products related to your links. Say you're selling camping equipment: you might link to a company that provides freeze-dried food or first-aid kits (if you are not already selling those products yourself). The main thing here is to post affiliate links that complement but do not compete with your products.

The final thing to consider when choosing your affiliate programs is how the links will affect the aesthetics of your website. A few affiliate links are fine, in fact, if they are links to products people want that are not available on your website, they can be quite welcome. If you were selling hair-care products and you knew the Farouk Chi hair straightener was extremely in-demand but was exclusively supplied by another company, your best alternative might be to provide an affiliate link to the exclusive supplier. However, an overload of links looks gimmicky, trashy, and hectic. If your site looks crummy, not only will people fail to click your links, but they probably won't buy any of your other products either.

Affiliate marketing is a legitimate way to make money. Some people have enough valuable informative content and efficient enough SEO that they make the entirety of their income off affiliate links and maybe a few ads. This is very difficult to do, so most people use an affiliate income to supplement their dropship-retailing website. You can experiment and see what works for you - just be aware that affiliate marketing isn't a cash cow you can milk at your convenience. It requires as much work as other e-businesses to be successful.

Chapter 13

Foreigners Rejoice: Dropship-Retailing From Outside the United States

Often, one of the biggest frustrations for people located outside the United States who are trying to start an online business is the fact that they're not American. You would think that e-commerce is global, but in fact many suppliers only want to work with Americans and many online businesses located in the States don't want to ship outside their own country. However, if you're not American, all is not lost – you can still dropship-retail. I'll let you in on a little secret – I'm actually Canadian myself, and I have prospered living and working in the United States for years. All you have to do is marry an American! I'm just kidding, you don't need to make matrimonial plans - you simply need to be a little more flexible than the average entrepeneur.

First, some background: dropshipping is a well-established supply-chain management system in the United States, but it is not quite as common in other countries yet. In the good old US of A, state laws help facilitate this kind of trade, but in places like Canada, the various provinces have tax strictures which can complicate matters. The good news is dropshipping is becoming increasingly prevalent in countries outside the US. If you're located in Canada, Australia, or the UK, rejoice because more and more suppliers are offering dropshipping in your respective countries.

So what are your options if you want to dropship-retail but you don't live in the US?

1. **Use local suppliers.**

Using local suppliers will allow you to bypass customs issues and avoid problems like American suppliers who demand an American Reseller's Permit and Tax ID Number. The downside to using only local suppliers is that your selection of suppliers and potential products will be more limited. If you can't find a supplier for your desired product, you might consider isolating the manufacturers you would like to work with, and ask if they would be willing to set up a dropshipping, wholesale, or affiliate program with you. Many companies are interested in the concept of dropshipping and might be willing to jump on the bandwagon if you could demonstrate how it would be beneficial to their business.

2. **Use American dropshippers.**

Some American dropshippers and wholesalers have no problem shipping outside the country, and will accept foreign documentation such as a Canadian business number in lieu of an American tax ID number. Canadians are particularly able to take advantage of American suppliers because the North American Free Trade Agreement (NAFTA) allows many products to be shipped duty-free if they are for customer's personal use (they usually have to be manufactured in either

Canada or the US, however). It is certainly worthwhile to look at the available American suppliers in addition to the ones located in your own country.

3. **Sell to Americans.**

If you are having a difficult time getting products shipped to customers in your own country, this may be the best solution for you. If you sell only to Americans, you can use practically any dropshipper you like, and you don't have to worry about cross-border hang-ups or local tax laws. You will still have to pay taxes on your income to your own government, but you won't have to worry about currency exchange or any of the other issues attendant with international sales. You may still encounter issues providing suppliers with documentation or setting up merchants accounts to receive your payments.

4. **Use Asian Suppliers**

As a person located outside the US, you may find that you can use cheap suppliers from countries that are not as accessible to Americans. For instance, if your country is close to China, you can use a wealth of inexpensive Asian suppliers that are more prickly for Americans to use due to the time and expensive of shipping something all the way from China to the US.

5. **Switch Products**

Remember, all would-be online entrepreneurs may have to switch their product idea if they can't find a good supplier.

This is even truer when your supplier pool is limited. Remember, the important thing is to sell a product you can make a profit on; it's not as important that you absolutely love equestrian gear or ice-cream makers or whatever it is you find an excellent supplier for.

I should interject here that if you are located in some exotic foreign locale, you should see that as a strength, not a weakness. I strongly recommend that you examine your local products when searching for something to sell online. Australian skim boards, Indian henna kits, Moroccan sandals, Balinese jewelry, these may seem like common products with a saturated market in your area, but that doesn't mean they're saturated online. I frequently receive requests from Americans who want to sell Australian skim boards, but the Australian suppliers won't dropship to them. This means that if you're Australian, you're actually in luck. Now, obviously shipping is a factor when selling to international customers, but there are many local products that you can sell on eBay or from a personal website to great effect.

I'm not going to lie and say that dropship-retailing is equally easy from any country, but I do believe that if you're flexible you can be successful. You may not be able to sell the product that you first had your heart set on, or use the supplier you first wanted, but there are doubtless other products and suppliers who will work just as well once you find them.

Chapter 14

Dot Your Ts and Cross Your Is: Checklist To Set Up Your Online
Business

If you jump into starting an online business without the necessary framework in place, you're probably going to hemorrhage money until you finally give up in totally frustration and bitterness, vowing never to do anything adventurous ever again. I've seen it happen time and again. However, with the proper planning, there's no reason your online business shouldn't be successful. To this end, the following is a checklist of things that need to be in place before you start paying for web designers and product sourcing.

1. Capital

This may be the most important prerequisite to starting an online business. If you only have a couple hundred dollars, you're going to spend that money and then be deadlocked because you won't have the cash to take the next step in setting up your online business. Now, you don't necessarily need to have thousands of dollars stashed under your mattress – you can apply for business loans or a line of credit to help get you started. The important thing to know is that you're probably not going to make money for the first couple of months, so you'll might need to keep your job as a supplementary source of income. Also, you're going to have to spend to obtain your Reseller's License and Tax ID Number, get your website set up and hosted, to find quality suppliers, and to fund Pay-Per-Click advertising to attract initial traffic to your website. There are both cheap and expensive ways of doing all these things, but they all cost something, and if you can't afford to pay for even the cheaper options, then you can't start a business right now, simple as that.

2. Business/Marketing Plan

I mentioned previously how important it is to have a business/marketing plan. You may need it to apply for business loans, find partners and investors, set up with suppliers, and you'll definitely need it to keep yourself on track. Since I've already described what a marketing plan should entail, I'm going to focus on your general business plan.

Your business plan is a formal statement of your business goals, why they are attainable, and your plan for reaching those goals. It will contain specific information about projected earnings, projected profit margins, branding/marketing targets, and operational plans. It will often include the results of market research, information about other companies you will be working with, and a number of graphs and supporting documents. There is no exact template for your business plan, but it should usually include a cover letter/summary, a statement of purpose, and a table of contents. The best way to get a feel for business plans is to check out some example plans from successful online businesses similar to yours. Over a hundred of these are available to view free   at   Bplans.com (http://www.bplans.com/sample_business_plans.cfm).

Once you have a general business plan written up, you can customize it for specific situations. For instance, if you are submitting your business plan to a bank for a loan, you'll want to address how you will pay back the loan (including what you will do if your business is not as financially successful as you expect it to be). If you're trying to attract an investor, you'll want to show how your current resources, growth opportunities, and competitive advantage will lead to a high exit valuation (profit return) for your investor.

Formal business plans should include copies of all pertinent documents, including balance sheets, loan applications, personal financial statements, tax returns for the last three years, copies of resumes for all major players in the company, copies of licenses and other legal documents, and letters of intent from suppliers, major accounts, etc.

You're not going to be able to "fake it" in a business plan. It needs to be a competent and convincing explanation of how and why your online business will succeed due to your unique idea, qualified talent, well-researched market, intelligent operations, and sufficient resources. If one or more of those areas are lacking, it's best that you're the first one to realize it while composing your business plan.

3. Reseller's Permit and Tax ID Number

For some reason, probably because filling out forms makes people want to bathe their eyeballs in vinegar, online business entrepreneurs are always trying to avoid getting their Reseller's Permit and Tax ID Number. They try to find suppliers who don't require it, or will only sell on eBay and never open their own website because they don't want to register their online business. Avoiding getting your Reseller's Permit and Tax ID Number isn't doing yourself any favors, in fact, it's a real detriment to your business. Getting the proper documentation should be the first step in starting your online business – you should do it immediately, not try to avoid it.

What is a Reseller's Permit?

A Reseller's Permit or Resale License is required if you sell or lease personal or tangible property: you need a Resellers Permit if you are a retailer or wholesaler of taxable items or services. The point of the Reseller's Permit is to avoid paying sales tax on items you are going to resell (you don't want to be charged taxes twice on the same item). Reseller's licenses vary state to state: you can either apply for one through the many, many companies offering their services online (for a fee), or you can download the form from your state revenue agency website.

What is a Tax ID Number?

A Federal Tax ID Number or "Employer Identification Number (EIN)" is a number assigned to your business by the IRS. Any business offering products or services that are taxed in any way needs to get this number. To get yours, simply apply online at the IRS website. It's very simple; in fact, you receive your number immediately and can download and print your confirmation notice. If you have any questions or concerns about Tax ID numbers, contact your nearest IRS Field office or call the IRS Business and Specialty Tax Hotline (800-829-4933).

Reasons why you need your Reseller's Permit and Tax ID Number:

Legitimate dropshippers and wholesalers require them.

If you want to work with a quality supplier, you need to provide them with your Reseller's Permit and/or Tax ID Number. Suppliers who don't ask for these are probably middlemen, not legitimate wholesalers or dropshippers. Thus, asking to work with a supplier who doesn't require the proper documentation is basically asking to work with a middleman.

Setting up your business properly allows you to take advantage of tax breaks.

Small business owners get a ton of tax breaks. I don't know why anyone who's not selling designer marijuana would operate their online business "under the radar", disqualifying themselves from all the government bursaries and benefits according to small businesses. As a business owner operating out of your own home, your phone, internet, and even a portion of your rent could qualify as write-offs, not to mention all the other expenses that come along with starting a new business.

You could be subject to fines and other penalties if you fail to register your business properly.

You can't legally sell property without a Reseller's Permit, and you'll probably have to file your taxes fraudulently at the end of the year without your Tax ID Number. It's a lot easier to set this stuff up in the first place than to scramble to get it later when an immediate need arises.

4. Ownership Structure

Another aspect of setting up your online business is deciding which ownership structure you want to use. Many people are drawn to the idea of registering their business as a corporation or LLC. This will separate you from your business so you will not necessarily be personally responsible for debts or legal judgments against your company. However, setting up your business in this way can be complicated and costly. Generally, I'd say it's not necessary, unless you're planning on amassing a mountain of debt or getting sued, and anyway it's something you can do further down the road if you so desire. However, you may decide it's the best option for you after speaking to a CPA or attorney.

The main types of business ownership are sole proprietorship, partnership, limited partnership, LLC, C Corporation and S Corporation. The following is a brief description of each:

Sole Proprietorship:

This is a one-person business not registered with the state. You are not required to register, file papers, or acquire documents. Basically, if you do nothing your online business with automatically be a sole proprietorship. In a sole proprietorship the business and owner are one and the same – you report your business income and losses on your personal tax return, which may or may not be a good thing for you. The negative to sole proprietorship is that you are personally responsible for business-related obligations like debts or settlements if you're sued.

Partnership:

A partnership is like a sole proprietorship in the sense that you don't file papers or documents. However, if you are entering into a partnership you would be wise to have some kind of contract since each partner is personally responsible for the entire amount of any business debt or claims. You'd also have a hard time recovering any resources your partner might make off with in the middle of the night if there was no contract in place.

Nobody enters into a partnership with someone they think is dishonest, yet people are ripped off by their business partners all the time. Even if your partner is your own mother, don't leave the door open to misunderstandings and future legal issues.

Limited Partnership:

Limited Partnerships are complicated and difficult to arrange (not to mention expensive), so this probably will not be the best avenue for your average online business entrepreneur. Basically, one person or company (the general partner) creates the business and receives investments from the limited partner(s). The general partner runs the day-to-day operations of the company and is responsible for all business debts. The limited partner has minimal input but also is not responsible for business debts or claims. Profit can be split in a variety of ways.

LLC:

An LLC (Limited Liability Company) is one of the more popular options for people starting an online business (it's certainly the option I receive the most questions about.) An LLC combines aspects of partnerships and corporations: its owners have limited liability for the company's debts and obligations like shareholders in a corporation, but its income and losses are passed through to the owners like in a partnership. It is much less formal and more flexible than a typical corporation. The benefits include separating your assets so you're protected in case your business gets sued. It also provides some tax breaks – you are only required to pay taxes on your earnings once instead of paying both corporate and individual taxes. The downside of an LLC versus a corporation is if a member of the LLC dies, leaves, or goes bankrupt, the LLC is usually dissolved. You might consider making your online business an LLC if you want to reap the tax benefits (this would be important if you expect your earnings for the year to be quite high).

To set up an LLC, you need to file Articles of Organization with you state (usually through the Secretary of State). You can hire an attorney to do this, or you can do it yourself (there are numerous do-it-yourself kits to help with this). When I have legal/business/accounting work, I like to do it myself, then hire a lawyer or CPA to check it over. That way I only have to pay for a little of their time, but I can be sure everything is correct before I file it, saving time and money in the long run.

Corporations:

A corporation is similar to an LLC: it is an entity that exists separate from the business owner, shielding owners and shareholders from company debt and obligations. To set one up, you must complete articles of incorporation, file them with the proper state authority, and pay the requisite fees. Unlike an LLC, if an owner dies or sells his interest, a corporation continues to exit until it is formally dissolves. A corporation can also issue stock, which helps attract outside investors.

A C corporation is a standard business corporation, while an S corporation has greater strictures but allows you to avoid double taxation. An S corporation is usually the choice of small business owners and entrepreneurs who want the legal protection of a corporation, but want to be taxed as sole proprietors or partners. The strictures such as "no more than 75 stockholders" and "only one class of stock can be issued" are not a problem for your average small-business owner. All stockholders/partners have to be US citizens or permanent residents, however.

This is a very basic business start-up checklist. You might have many other ducks you want to get in a row before you really start your online business, including finding investment partners, clearing out a space for a home office, hiring a lackey, etc.

Conclusion:

Now that you're armed with the basic knowledge necessary to start an online business, it's time to spread your little wings and fly. If there's one piece of advice I can leave you with, it's this: don't be afraid to change, to start over, to try again. Countless business owners fail at their first venture or their first five ventures before going on to found multi-million dollar companies. One of the most obvious examples of this is Donald Trump, who went bankrupt multiple times before riding the wave of his current success. In point of fact, you'll find that most people operating a successful business today (particularly online) have at least one failed venture in their past.

Not all of these failures are disastrous – sometimes you break even, or make a small profit, or lose only a small amount. That is the one of the beauties of online business – you won't be stuck with a year-long lease in an expensive office building, or a costly billboard or YellowPages ad draining your pocketbook. If your online business does not have the capacity to make money that you thought it did, you can cut your PPC ads and stop your web hosting immediately. Or even better, you can alter your strategy. You don't have to start from scratch with an online business – you could change your product line, tweak your website, switch your business name. Online business is flexible, and if you too are flexible, winning to learn from your mistakes, and tenacious enough to try again on a different tack, there's no reason why you shouldn't prosper in the future.

Setbacks and hardships only become failures when you don't learn from your mistakes, or when you give up entirely. I hope that you won't give up. You can always learn new skills, brainstorm new tactics, and overcome whatever road blocks have tripped you in the past. The ability to evolve and keep pressing forward is what separates the Donald Trumps of the world from all those other guys you've never heard of.

Appendix

EBay Vocabulary

If you've ever tried to sell something on eBay, you may have felt like you had to speak a foreign language just to read the instructions. To help you take advantage of eBay's many features, I've included a kind of Cliff's Notes, or as those of you who struggled through high school Spanish may prefer *not* to think of it, a Vocab Page.

EBay Terms and Phrases:

About Me: This is an eBay page you can create to inform your customers of your products and selling terms and conditions. Make sure you have a comprehensive About Me page, because most people who bother to look here are probably shy buyers, and need the security and encouragement your profile can convey.

Advanced Search: This is an important search function you should use every time before you list a product. It allows you to search for items by seller, item number, and title and description, but most importantly it allows you to search completed listings. By seeing what your particular product has sold for recently, you can make sure that you are likely to get a similar price. For instance, if you're planning to dropship an electric train set that will cost you $138, but you see similar sets are only selling for around $90, you know not to waste your $2 posting fee.

Announcements Board: This is an online bulletin board where eBay posts information and updates including policy changes. Check this board regularly to make sure you're not missing crucial information.

Apps: EBay recently added a number of apps or programs that you can use in conjunction with your eBay account. Some are free and others have monthly, annual, or one-time fees. They include accounting, shipping and packaging, and marketing software.

Auction-Style Listing: This is a listing where the seller offers an item for customers to bid on. The seller sets the starting price, and then potential buyers bid, just like at a regular auction. There is a set time-period when bidding will end, and whoever has the highest bid at that point gets the item. (You can set a reserve price to make sure you get at least a minimum amount for your item – though you will have to pay eBay a percentage of your reserve.)

Average Selling Price (ASP): This is the average price for all items in a particular category sold during a particular time-frame. This is what you'll be checking with an advanced search before you post any products.

Best Offer: If you are listing products in the Fixed-Price format, you can add the Best Offer feature. It allows bidders to submit a Best Offer price, and if the seller accepts it within 48 hours, the listing immediately closes. A Best Offer is binding, just like a bid (meaning once it is made, the buyer has to follow through if it's accepted.)

Buy It Now (BIN): Whether you are selling your item auction-style or in a Fixed-Price listing, you can offer a Buy It Now option. This allows customers to purchase the product immediately for a set price without waiting for the auction to end. Adding a Buy It Now price can help you get more sales quickly, but it puts a cap on how much your product will sell for. Thus, if you are selling an item that may be bid up very high, it's probably not a good idea.

Certified Solution Provider: This term refers to third-party software developers who offer programs to use in conjunction with eBay. They are bound by criteria and compliance standards set by eBay, and their programs are often quite useful. The eBay Apps would be an example of this kind of software.

Closed Item Listing: This indicates that a listing that has ended. If the item sold, there will be information provided about payments, shipping and the buyer. If it's your closed item listing, you can also find the info in My EBay.

Completed Listings Search: This is what you'll be doing on the "Advanced Search" page to research the closing sale prices of products similar to yours.

Confirmed Address: This is an address considered safe and reliable by PayPal (usually confirmed by something like a credit card billing address match). You should know that the only sales protected from chargebacks by PayPal are those sent by confirmed mail to a confirmed address. If you ship to anyone else, you do so at your own risk (they could easily claim they never received the package and even if you have the delivery confirmation, PayPal will probably charge it back – even if the money is already in your bank account.)

Dropshipping: You can dropship on eBay just like you can from a personal website. You simply post the item on eBay, and once it sells, you order it from your wholesaler / manufacturer / distributor and have it mailed directly to your customer. You keep the difference in the price.

Dutch Auction: Synonymous with a Multiple Item Auction, this means a seller has two or more identical items offered in the same auction-style listing.

EBay Shipping Calculator: This is something you insert into your listing so buyers can tell how much shipping is going to cost them.

EBay Store: Once you've gotten a minimum feedback rating of 20 and you are ready to handle multiple listings, you may want to switch to an eBay store.   This will allow you to sell add-ons and show inventory. You'll also have more customizable pages and banner ads that will help bring business your way.

EBay Toolbar: This is a tool you can download to your web browser to help you keep track of your items and protect your account even when you're not on eBay's site.

Featured Listing: You have the option to pay more to have your listings showcased in the "Featured" sections at the top of the listings pages.

Feedback: After every sale, your buyer has the option of rating you positively, negatively or neutrally. (They give a numerical rating and can leave a short comment). Likewise, you the seller can leave feedback on your buyer. Feedback ratings are checked by other potential buyers judging whether they want to do business with you, so make sure you do whatever it takes to keep your customers happy and avoid negative feedback.

Final Value Fee (FVF): This is the percentage of your product's selling price that will be paid to eBay.

Final Value Fee Credit: Sometimes you can request a Final Value Fee Credit, like if your buyer backs out and doesn't buy the item after all.

Fixed Price: A set price for selling items immediately without bidding.

Flat Shipping Rate: When you post your shipping costs, you can either offer a shipping cost calculated according to where the buyer lives, or a flat rate that is the same no matter where your buyer lives. If you go with flat shipping rates, you can offer promotions like discounted or free shipping with a certain volume sale (these kinds of marketing techniques work much better when you're selling from an eBay store, not single items).

Formats: You can post your eBay listings in a variety of formats to customize your marketing techniques. Some formats work better for certain products. For instance, you can use auction-style for products that are likely to have a lot of competitive bidding to drive the price up. You may prefer to use the Fixed-Price format for items that tend to sell at a set price, (this is especially helpful if you have multiple items of the same type that you wish to sell quickly).

Gallery Picture: This refers to the thumbnail picture of your item that will appear next to your listing in the search results.

Gift Icon: If you think your product would make a great gift, you can add this icon to your listing to help promote it. It costs 25 cents, but is particularly helpful around holidays. If you choose to use this icon, you should probably be ready to offer gift wrapping, personal messages, express shipping, gift receipts (with no price on them), etc.

Gross Merchandise Volume (GMV): This is a measure of total sales of all your active listings or all items sold.

ID Verify: ID Verify is a check system eBay has put in place to help prove the identity of sellers. It is to your benefit to get ID Verify on your account because it adds a security icon to your profile and helps customers to trust you. EBay also requires it before they'll allow you to add Buy It Now to your listings, sell in Fixed-Price format, and bid above $15 000. All you have to do is pay $5.00 and provide proof of your identity. It's only valid until your name, address, or phone number change, so make sure that information is accurate on your account first.

Immediate Payment: If a buyer purchases a product from you at the Buy It Now price, you can require them to pay immediately through PayPal. You probably won't need to do this often, but you might want to with very high demand or time-sensitive items (like tickets to a football game).

Insertion Fee: This is the fee eBay charges to post a listing, and it's non-refundable.

Item Listing: This is the description of your product that you post on eBay to entice customers to buy, and it usually includes photos, product features, shipping info, etc. The better your listing, the more likely you are to make a sale, and the higher your closing price will be. Learning to write a good listing is crucial.

Item Specifics: Item Specifics is a feature where you can add details about your product to help people find your listing. Customers using the Product Finder to search for specific features like "size 10" or "Gucci" will be directed to your shoes instead of a general list of thousands of pairs of shoes. You should definitely use the Item Specifics to make your product more visible.

Learning Center: These are videos and tutorials to explain the eBay process. If you're an eBay newbie, you should probably brush up on the rules and procedures at the Learning Center before you jump into the deep end of the pool.

Matching Categories: You'll want to post your listing according to category (probably in a couple of categories). That way when customers search for "dresses" or "doll clothes", your listing will pop up in that category.

Mint: You can use this descriptor to indicate that your item is in perfect condition. It's often used with comic books, antiques, old coins, etc. But it better be true if you use it.

My eBay: Everyone on eBay has a My eBay page. It shows all your activity on eBay, including your listings, purchases, and sales. It's a way to keep track of what you're doing.

Natural Search: When you perform a natural search, you search through all unpaid results based on relevance. Conversely, you can perform a paid search where you would be given results the sellers have paid for placing in.

Online Dispute Resolution (ODR): If you have a disagreement or dispute with someone you deal with on eBay, you can request mediation by eBay's third-party provider SquareTrade.

Opening Value: Synonymous with starting price. You can start your auction-style listings as low as 99 cents, but then you risk your product selling for, say, $6 instead of the $120 it's worth. You could start your auction higher, say at $99, or put a reserve price of $120 so you don't have to accept any bids lower than that, but then you will have to pay a percentage of the price to eBay. If you are positive that your product will sell for a good price, you might want to put a low opening value, but you have to consider the risk carefully. Low opening values do help create interest, so factor that in.

Paid Search: This is a search performed where the results are not ranked by relevance, but rather prominently feature products that have paid for placement in the search engine.

PayPal: This is a payment service where buyers can pay the seller through PayPal with credit cards, from their bank account, or with an accumulated balances from their own sales. PayPal is convenient for buyers because it allows them flexible payment options and is quite secure (they don't have to give their credit card info, etc., to a random seller). It's also convenient for sellers because most buyers like it, and the seller can accept credit card payments without a merchant account. However, while PayPal is free for the buyer, it costs the seller a percentage of the sale price (usually between 1.9-2.9 percent).

PayPal Buyer Credit: PayPal Buyer Credit is like a credit card, only the funds are available through PayPal. Like a credit card, you can shop and run up a balance, then make small monthly payments on the balance. Also like a credit card, it charges you interest. I'm not really sure why you would want this, since it's more restrictive than a credit card (you can only use it for purchases online), and there is no rewards program like most credit cards have. There are some promotional financing offers that might be attractive, I suppose (no interest if purchases over a certain amount are paid within a certain time period, etc.). Acceptance into this program is dependent on your credit rating and it is currently only available to Americans.

PayPal Buyer Protection: When you use PayPal to make a purchase on eBay, you are automatically protected from fraud up to $2,000 if your purchase is off a qualified listing.

PayPal Seller Protection Policy: Likewise, when you sell via PayPal you're protected from chargebacks. However, this only applies if you follow the Seller Protection Policy. This means you can only ship to confirmed addresses using a verifiable shipping method. If you're a PowerSeller, you can get Expanded Seller Protection so your protection volume is unlimited and you can ship internationally.

PowerSeller: This is a term applied to eBay sellers who sell a high volume each month and maintain a 98 percent or better positive rating. PowerSellers are further rated from Bronze to Titanium according to their sales volumes.

Private Listing: In a private listing, the bidders' user IDs are not visible on the listing page. You would definitely want to use this kind of listing for, say, adult items.

Prohibited Items: These are items which are not allowed to be sold on eBay. If you sell prohibited items, you risk having your account suspended or canceled. You can find a list of prohibited items under Rules & Policies in the "Help Topics" section on eBay.

Proxy Bidding: If you prefer, you can enter the maximum amount you would bid for an item and eBay will automatically place bids for you until it hits the maximum. This allows you to remain the top bidder without you logging on and bidding every few minutes. (Don't be confused – if no one else bids, your bid won't shoot up to the maximum).

Reseller Marketplace: PowerSellers can use this section of eBay to purchase products for resale.

Reserve Price: When you're posting an item for sale, you can enter a hidden minimum price below which you won't sell the product. This means that you are not required to accept bids lower than your minimum price. However, you are required to pay eBay a portion of your reserve price if you make a sale.

Restricted Items: Restricted items have special rules for resale, but they are not prohibited. Again, you can check the rules for these kinds of items by going to Rules & Policies and looking in the "Help Topics" section on eBay.

Sales Reports: The Sales Reports are a tracking system to help you monitor your eBay business. The reports include information on your sales, completed listings, your successful listing percentage, average sale price, your eBay and PayPal fees, and so on and so forth. It's a free subscription.

Search Optimization: Like with your website, you need to perform search optimization to make your eBay listings and eBay store visible. The best way to optimize your listings is through efficient and appropriate keyword use in titles and descriptions. EBay stores require more complicated optimization, much like a website, including keywords, backlinks, fresh copy, etc.

Second Chance Offer: You can extend a Second Chance Offer to bidders who didn't win the item you had for sale. This would be appropriate if the winner backed out of the purchase or failed to pay for the item, or if you had duplicate items you wanted to sell (you could also sell duplicates through a Multiple Item auction).

Security & Resolution Center: This is an eBay resource with safety and security tips. You can also find assistance for eBay confrontations and disagreements here.

Seller Dashboard: This is the part of My eBay where you can find account details like your 30-day rolling average DSR score (Detailed Seller Rating score) and your PowerSeller discount eligibility.

Selling Manager and Selling Manager Pro: These are tools that you can use to perform your listing and sales activities from one location in My eBay. They're supposed to save you time and help you stay organized.

Shill Bidding: Shill bidding means placing bids on your own items to raise the price in auction-style listings. This is totally dishonest and forbidden on eBay (it's even illegal in some places). It's also wrong if you're doing it on your friends' listings. Any time you're bidding to raise the price, not because you actually have an interest in purchasing the product, you are shill bidding.

Shipping Center: This is a page on eBay where you can print labels, order boxes, and organize your shipping, but you certainly don't have to use it. If you already have your own packing and shipping system that works for you, or are dropshipping, you don't need to use eBay's system.

Sniping: This refers to deliberately placing a bid in the closing minutes or seconds of a listing. It's not actually forbidden on eBay. Some people do it manually, and some people use sniping programs. You can also place proxy bids to help you snipe.

Solutions Directory: This is a directory of the eBay and third-party software which is compliant with eBay standards and is supposed to help you run your eBay business smoothly. Some of the software is free, some has fees.

Spoof Email: This is email that appears to be from eBay or PayPal, but is really a phishing scheme. (A phishing scheme is a phony request for financial or personal information). Don't respond to these emails and report them to spoof@ebay.com or spoof@paypal.com. Real emails from eBay and PayPal won't ask for personal or financial information – that would be a non-secure way to request the information.

Starting Price: This is the opening price for an auction-style listing. Unless you have a reserve price, your product could conceivably sell for the starting price or a tiny bit more, so unless you have a popular product you are positive will attract aggressive bidding, you'll probably want your starting price to equal the lowest price you would accept for your product, or include a reserve price.

Turbo Lister: This is a free tool you can use on eBay to list many items at once.

Unpaid Item: If your buyer commits to purchasing an item but doesn't provide payment, you need to report the unpaid item. This will prevent you having to pay the Final Value Fee. To report an unpaid item, you'll first have to speak with the Resolution Center. If you can't fix the problem working with them, you report your unpaid item by going to My eBay, clicking on Sold, finding the listing, and selecting "Resolve A Problem" from the pull-down menu. A Resolve a Problem form will appear: on that form you select "I sold an item and haven't received my payment yet", then click Continue. You sign into your account, and the "Report an unpaid item case" form will appear. You'll have to put in your number from the Resolution Center, then submit your case details. Only after the unpaid item is reported can you re-list it or make a Second Chance Offer to somebody else.

Verified Rights Owner (VERO) Program: If someone lists an item on eBay that is actually your intellectual property, you can use this program to request the removal of the listing.

Want It Now: EBay buyers can post in this format to let sellers know that they're looking for a particular item. For example, if you wanted to purchase a pair of vintage aviator sunglasses, you could post a Want It Now listing stating the details of the sunglasses you're looking for. Sellers could then make offers.

About the Authors

Steve Sonnenberg

Steve Sonnenberg is a young entrepreneur who started his first online company as a full-time student at Utah Valley University in 2004. While attending school, he was the recipient of two nationwide entrepreneur awards from Loyola Marymount University. He is married with four children. Steve began his career as an online business consultant. He personally mentored thousands of aspiring online entrepreneurs from 1999 to 2004. In 2004 Steve created his first online business, and has since employed over 400 people. Before the age of thirty, Steve has begun to net over one million dollars a year.

Leah Darrow

Leah Darrow is a blog, business, and fiction writer. She graduated from Athabasca University in 2008. She is a new mom, and currently lives in Utah with her husband Ryan.

Made in the USA
Lexington, KY
16 February 2014